Essentials of C++

A Lab Course Through Arrays

Nell Dale
University of Texas, Austin

JONES AND BARTLETT PUBLISHERS
Sudbury, Massachusetts
BOSTON   TORONTO   LONDON   SINGAPORE

World Headquarters
Jones and Bartlett Publishers
40 Tall Pine Drive
Sudbury, MA 01776
978-443-5000
info@jbpub.com
www.jbpub.com

Jones and Bartlett Publishers Canada
2100 Bloor St. West
Suite 6-272
Toronto, ON M6S 5A5
CANADA

Jones and Bartlett Publishers International
Barb House, Barb Mews
London W6 7PA
UK

ISBN: 0-7637-0858-5

Printed in the United States of America
03 02 01 00   10 9 8 7 6 5 4 3 2

Contents

Preface

Rationale for This Text

For the last 18 years the introductory computer science course has been taught mostly in Pascal. However, over the last 4 or 5 years schools have started to replace Pascal with other languages, such as C++. When Pascal was the first language, we could cover the entire language in one semester. The second semester could then focus on using and building alternate implementations of the ADTs: lists, stacks, queues, trees, and (perhaps) graphs. Where CS1 ended and CS2 began was clear. Now this distinction is no longer clear.[1] In fact, the content of CS2 is no longer uniform.

1. Schools that use another language, such as Scheme or Miranda, in their CS1 course and switch to C++ in the second semester need to cover C++ as a second language before beginning the traditional data structures coverage.
2. Schools that use C++ for both CS1 and CS2 and assume no previous background do not get as far as they could in Pascal. Thus the transition between the two semesters is somewhere about the end of arrays.
3. Schools that use C++ for both courses but assume that the students have had some programming before taking CS1 are able to go faster and push the transition point deeper into C++.

This lab manual is designed to be used in the first situation: to quickly teach the essentials of C++ to students who know another programming language. "Essentials of C++" are defined to be the minimum subset of C++ through arrays that a student needs for CS2. This manual can also be used as a review for students whose backgrounds are weak.

Why a Laboratory Approach?

C and later C++ were designed for systems programming. Systems programmers are assumed to know what they mean and mean what they say. Therefore C++ has very little run-time error checking and compiles some very weird code. Beginning students, on the other hand, often do not know what they mean and even more often do not mean what they say. Hence it is essential that students understand the syntax and semantics of each construct as they go along. Closed laboratory activities seem an ideal way to make this happen.

Closed Laboratories in Computer Science

The Denning Report[2] introduced the term *closed laboratories* without defining exactly what they were. At least four different definitions subsequently surfaced.

1. A scheduled time when students work on their programming assignments under supervision.

---

[1] The ideas expressed here were presented by the author in a panel at the ACM/SIGCSE 1998 Technical Symposium in Atlanta, Georgia.

[2] Denning, P. J. (chair) "Computing as a Discipline" *Communications of the ACM*, Vol. 32, No. 1, pp. 9-23.

2. A scheduled drill and practice time when students work on mini-problems under supervision.
3. The use of specially prepared laboratory materials where students interact with the computer as they would a microscope or Bunsen burner. The labs should help the student discover principles and solutions under supervision. This definition is closest to the spirit of the Denning Report.
4. A combination of two or more of the above.

With the publication of the Curriculum '91[1] report, laboratory exercises were suggested for many of the knowledge units. However a precise definition of what constituted a closed laboratory activity was not included. And, in fact, many of the activities suggested could be done equally well in a nonsupervised (or open) setting.

Laboratory activities as defined in this manual are a combination of definitions 2 and 3.

Open versus Closed Laboratories

Although the Denning Report and Curriculum '91 imply that laboratory exercises should be done under supervision, we do not feel that this is essential. Our view is that closed laboratory exercises are valuable for two reasons: the exercises themselves and the extra contact time with a faculty member or a teaching assistant. If a closed laboratory environment is not an option, the students can still benefit from working the exercises on their own.

Organization of the Manual

The material is broken into four chapters. If the students already know how to program or if the text is being used as a review for students whose background is weak, each chapter can be covered in a week. The pace is very fast, but the idea behind this text is to prepare students quickly for the CS2 material.

Each chapter contains three types of activities: reading material, laboratory activities, and suggested programs to be done from scratch. The reading material includes paper and pencil self-check exercises, the answers to which are included in the back of the manual. The laboratory activities are broken into lessons, each of which represents a concept covered in the chapter. Each lesson is broken into exercises that thoroughly demonstrate the concept. The suggested programs are a collection of outside programming assignments appropriate for each chapter.

The laboratory activities are designed to take approximately two hours, the usual time for a closed laboratory. However an instructor can tailor the chapter to the level of the class by only assigning a partial set of exercises or by shortening the time allowed.

A selection of programming projects are listed in Programs from Scratch. We do not suggest that all of them be assigned. In most cases one should be sufficient, unless there are several related problems.

If the manual is not being used in a closed-laboratory setting, an instructor can assign all or a selection of the activities to be done independently (see the section on "Flexibility" below). In either a closed or open setting, many of the laboratory and programming activities can be done in groups.

---

[1]Tucker, A. B. (Ed.) "Computing Curricula 1991: Report of the ACM/IEEE-CS Joint Curriculum Task Force. Final Draft, December 17. ACM Order Number 201910. IEEE Computer Society Press Order Number 2220.

Theoretical Basis for the Activities

The decision to break each chapter in three types of activities is based on the work of Benjamin Bloom, who developed a taxonomy of six increasingly difficult levels of achievement in the cognitive domain.[1] In developing the activities for this manual, we combined Bloom's six categories into three. These categories are defined below in terms of the concrete example of learning an algorithm (or language-related construct).

Recognition The student can trace the algorithm and determine what the output should be for a given data set (no transfer).

Generation The student can generate a very similar algorithm (near transfer).

Projection The student can modify the algorithm to accomplish a major change (far transfer), can apply the algorithm in a different context, can combine related algorithms, and can compare algorithms.

The paper and pencil self-check activities are at the recognition level. Most of the laboratory activities are at the generation level with a few projection-level activities included where appropriate. The complete programs are projection-level activities.

The activities are also influenced by the work of Kolb and others on how students learn.[2] The more actively involved students are in the learning process, the more they learn. Reading and writing are forms of active involvement. Therefore many of the exercises ask the students to write explanations of what happened. Just watching a program run and looking at the answer is a passive activity, but having to write the answer down transforms the exercise into an active one.

Flexibility

Essentials of C++: A Laboratory Course Through Arrays is designed to allow the instructor maximum flexibility. Each chapter has an assignment cover sheet that provides a checklist in tabular form. The first column of the table lists the chapter activities, in the second column students check which activities have been assigned, in the third column they record what output is to be turned in, and the fourth column is for the instructor to use for grading. The pages are perforated so that students can easily tear out sheets to turn in.

---

[1]Bloom, Benjamin *Taxonomy of Educational Objectives: Handbook I: Cognitive Domain*. New York: David McKay, 1956.

[2]Svinicki, Marilla D., and Dixon Nancy M. "The Kolb Model Modified for Classroom Activities" *College Teaching*, Vol. 35, No. 4, Fall, pp. 141-146.

Essentials of C++: A Lab Course Through Arrays **Program Disk**

Jones and Bartlett Publishers offers free to students and instructors a program disk with the complete programs found in *Essentials of C++: A Lab Course Through Arrays*. The program disk is available through the Jones and Bartlett World Wide Web site on the Internet. *

Download Instructions

1. Connect to the Jones and Bartlett student diskette home page (www.jbpub.com/disks/).

2. Choose *Essentials of C++: A Lab Course Through Arrays*.

3. Follow the instructions for downloading and saving the *Essentials of C++: A Lab Course Through Arrays* data disk.

4. If you need assistance downloading a Jones and Bartlett student diskette, please send email to help@jbpub.com.

*Downloading the *Essentials of C++: A Lab Course Through Arrays* program disk via the Jones and Bartlett home page requires access to the Internet and a World Wide Web browser such as Netscape Navigator or Microsoft Internet Explorer. Instructors at schools without Internet access may call 800-832-0034 and request a copy of the program disk. Jones and Bartlett grants adopters of *Essentials of C++: A Lab Course Through Arrays* the right to duplicate copies of the program disk or to store the files on any stand-alone computer or network.

Acknowledgments

No author writes in a vacuum. There is always formal and informal feedback from colleagues. Thanks to those of you in my department who patiently answered "by the way" questions about C++. Thanks also to the following colleagues who wrote formal reviews of the manuscript for *A Laboratory Course in C++*, upon which this manuscript is based: Mary D. Medley, Augusta College; Susan Wallace, University of North Florida; Paul Ross, Millersville University of Pennsylvania; Jeanine Ingber, University of New Mexico, Albequerque; James C. Miller, Bradley University; Ed Korntved, Northwest Nazarene College; Charles Dierbach, Towson State University; Mansar Zand, University of Nebraska, Omaha and Mark Headington, University of Wisconsin, La Crosse.A special thanks to David Teague, Western Carolina University, and Robert Strader, Stephen F. Austin State University, who reviewed this abbreviated and reorganized version.

Getting Started with C++

OBJECTIVES

- To be able to write simple arithmetic expressions to accomplish a specified task.
- To be able to convert a value from one numeric type to another numeric type.
- To be able to determine when implicit conversion of a value in one type to a value in another type occurs.
- To be able to write output statements that format data in specified ways.
- To be able to use value-returning library functions.
- To be able to determine how data must be input in order for a program to run correctly.
- To be able to examine the input data to a program and the results and deduce the form of the input statements.
- To be able to take a program that extracts data from the keyboard and change it to extract data from a file.
- To be able to construct input and output statements that take their input from a file and send their output to a file.
- To be able to debug a program that inputs data from the keyboard and a file.

C++ Syntax and Semantics

There are two basic parts to a C++ program: (1) instructions to the C++ preprocessor and compiler and (2) instructions that describe the processing to be performed. However, before we can describe these instructions, we must have a way of naming things so that we can tell the compiler about them and describe what we want to have done to them. We name things (data types, data objects, and actions) by giving them an identifier. An identifier is made up of letters, numbers, and underscores, but it must begin with a letter or an underscore. We use the words identifier and name interchangeably.

Beware: C++ is case sensitive. This means that Value, VALUE, value, and vaLue are four separate identifiers. In fact, we can construct 32 distinct identifiers from these five letters by varying the capitalization.

Program Structure

Let's examine the following C++ program. We have numbered the lines so that we can discuss them.

```
1.   // Program Lunch calculates the number of calories in
2.   // a cheese sandwich.

3.   #include <iostream.h>

4.   const int BREAD = 63;       // calories in a slice of bread
5.   const int CHEESE = 106;     // calories in a slice of cheese
6.   const int MAYONNAISE = 49;  // calories in mayonnaise
7.   const int PICKLES = 25;     // calories in pickles

8.   int main()
9.   {
10.      int totalCalories;

11.      totalCalories = 2 * BREAD + CHEESE
                            + MAYONNAISE + PICKLES;
12.      cout << "There were " << totalCalories;
13.      cout << " calories in my lunch yesterday." << endl;
14.      cout << "What is for lunch today?" << endl;
15.      return 0;
16.  }
```

Lines 1 and 2 begin with a double slash (//) and are ignored by the translation system. Such lines are called comments and are meant for the reader of the program. They tell the user what the program is going to do. Comments begin with // and extend to the end of the line. Another way of entering comments into the program is to insert them between /* and */. Comments between /* and */ can extend across any number of lines.

Line 3 is a directive to the C++ preprocessor. The preprocessor scans the program for lines beginning with a hash mark (#). The words "**include <iostream.h>**" tell the preprocessor to insert the contents of the file **iostream.h** in place of the directive. The angle brackets around the file name indicate that the file is in the standard *include directory*. This file includes constant, variable, and function declarations needed by the program.

Lines 4 through 7 instruct the compiler to assign the identifier on the left of the equal sign a place in memory and to store the value on the right of the equal sign in that place. A constant declaration is made up of the reserved word `const` followed by the data type identifier `int`. `int` says that the value to be stored in the constant is an integer value. The data type identifier is followed by the name to be given to the constant: in this case, `BREAD`. The constant name is followed by an equal sign and the value to be stored there. By convention, most C++ programmers use all uppercase for constant identifiers.

Line 8 contains the words that begin the executable part of the program—that is, the part that contains statements describing what you want the program to do. A function performs an action and returns a result. The data type identifier `int` says that the value returned by function `main` is an integer. The compiler knows that `main` is a function because it is followed by a pair of parentheses. All C++ programs must have an `int` function `main`. Line 9 contains only one character: the left brace (`{`). This character begins a block that is the body of the function. The right brace (`}`) on line 16 is the closing brace of the block; it ends the body of the function. The body of the function contains the statements that are translated by the compiler and executed when the program is run.

Line 10 contains the declaration of `totalCalories`, an integer variable. The compiler assigns a memory location to `totalCalories`. Nothing is stored in `totalCalories` yet. When values are stored there, they must be values of type `int`.

Line 11 is an assignment statement. The expression on the right side of the equal sign is evaluated, and the result is stored in the variable whose identifier is on the left of the equal sign. Therefore, 306 is stored in `totalCalories`.

Lines 12 through 14 cause information to be written on the screen. `cout`, which is defined in file `<iostream.h>`, is a predefined variable that denotes an *output stream*. An output stream is just what it sounds like: a stream of characters sent to some output device. The operator `<<` (double less-than signs) is called the *insertion operator*. The stream of characters described on the right of the insertion operator is sent to the output stream named on the left of the insertion operator. Let's look at line 12 (repeated below) in detail.

```
12.      cout << "There were "  << totalCalories;
```

The collection of characters that appear between the double quotes is called a *string*. The leftmost insertion operator sends the string to `cout`; that is, the characters that make up the string are printed on the screen. The next insertion operator sends the value stored in variable `totalCalories` to `cout`.

Line 13 has two insertion operators: the first sends a string to `cout` and the second sends a special feature called a *manipulator* to the output stream. `endl` is a manipulator that tells the output stream to go to a new line by writing the end-of-line marker. Thus, anything written after this statement begins on the next line of output. Line 14 sends another string and the end-of-line manipulator to `cout`.

We said that the executable part of the program is `int` function `main`. Because `main` is an `int` function, it must return an integer value. Line 15 says to return the value zero. By convention, `main` returns zero when the program executes with no errors. Line 16 ends function `main` and thus the program. The output from this program is:

```
There were 306 calories in my lunch yesterday.
What is for lunch today?
```

Data Types

A data type is a set of values and a set of operations on these values. In the preceding program, we used the data type identifier `int`. In the discussion we called `totalCalories` (declared as type `int`) an integer variable. In C++ there are four integral types that can be used to refer to an integer value (whole numbers with no fractional parts). These types are `char`, `short`, `int`, and `long` and are intended to represent integers of different sizes. Although the actual number of bits used to represent each of these types varies from one computer to another, the number of digits that can be represented increases from `char` (the smallest) to `long` (the largest). The set of values for each of these integral data types is the range of numbers from the smallest value that can be represented through the largest value that can be represented. The operations on these values are the standard arithmetic operations allowed on integer values.

   `float`, `double`, and `long double` are data type identifiers that refer to floating point numbers; that is, numbers with a whole and a fractional part. Again, the set of values is defined by the range of the minimum value through the maximum value that can be represented. The operations are the standard arithmetic operators allowed on decimal values.

   In addition to the standard arithmetic operators, C++ provides an *increment* operator and a *decrement* operator. The increment operator `++` adds one to its operand; the decrement operator `--` subtracts one from its operand.

   Data type `char`, the smallest integral data type, has an additional use: to describe one alphanumeric character. Each machine has a character set made up of all the alphanumeric characters that can be represented. If we need to represent a character in a program, we enclose it in single quotes. The following are seven alphanumeric characters available in all character sets.

```
'A'   'a'   '0'   ' '   '*'   '$'   '9'
```

Although arithmetic operations are defined on alphanumeric characters because they are type `char` (an integral type), such operations would not make any sense to us at this point. However, there is a collating sequence defined on each character set, so we can ask if one character comes before another character. Fortunately, the uppercase letters, the lowercase letters, and the digits are in order in all character sets. The relationship between these groups varies, however. We discuss manipulating `char` data in Chapter 4.

Operator Symbols

Here is a table of the C++ equivalent of the standard arithmetic operators and the other operators defined in this chapter.

Operator	*Meaning*
+	Unary plus
-	Unary minus
+	Addition
-	Subtraction
*	Multiplication

/	Floating point operands: floating point result
	Integer operands: quotient
	Mixed operands: floating point result
%	Modulus (remainder from integer division, operands must be integral)
+ +	Increment by one; can be prefix or postfix
- -	Decrement by one; can be prefix or postfix
=	Assignment; evaluate expression on right and store in the variable named on the left
< <	Insertion; insert the characters (if a string) or the value (if a variable or constant) into the output stream named on the left of the first insertion operator

Words and Symbols with Special Meanings

Certain words have predefined meanings within the C++ language; these are called *reserved words*. For example, the names of data types are reserved words. In program **Lunch**, there are three reserved words: `const`, `int`, and `return`. `const` directs the compiler to set up a constant; `int` is a data type identifier for an integral value; and `return` signals the end of the function and usually sends back a value.

A hash mark followed by the word `include` and a file name is an instruction to the C++ preprocessor. It directs the preprocessor to insert the contents of the file into the program at that point.

Two slashes (`//`) signal that the characters from that point to the end of the line are comments and are to be ignored by the compiler. Characters written between `/*` and `*/` are also comments and ignored by the compiler.

The statements that define constants (lines 4 through 7) and variables (line 10) are called *declarations*. A C++ program is made up of declarations and one or more function definitions. A function definition is made up of a heading and a block. Line 8 is the function heading. The block begins with the left brace on line 9 and ends with the right brace on line 16.

Semicolons terminate statements in the C++ language. There are ten semicolons in program **Lunch**, so there are ten statements in the program: four statements in the declaration section and six statements in the block of function **main**.

✓ Paper and Pencil Self Check #1

Examine the following program and answer Exercises 1 through 5.

```
// Program Schedule prints a daily schedule with the
// amount of time spent on each task.
#include <iostream.h>
const int DRESS = 45;
const int EAT   = 30;
const int DRIVE = 30;
const int CLASS = 60;
```

```
int main()
{
    int   totalMinutes;

    totalMinutes = DRESS + 3*EAT + 2*DRIVE + 4*CLASS;
    cout << "You spend "  << totalMinutes / 60
         << " hours and " << totalMinutes % 60
         << " minutes on scheduled activities."
         << endl;
    return 0;
}
```

Exercise 1:   What is written by program **Schedule**?

Exercise 2:   List the identifiers that are defined in program **Schedule**.

Exercise 3:   Which of these identifiers are named constants?

Exercise 4:   List the literal constants.

Exercise 5:   List the identifiers that are defined in **<iostream.h>**.

Arithmetic Expressions, Function Calls, and Output

In the last section, we showed how identifiers are constructed and explained how they name data types, data objects, and actions. We used the following two statements.

```
const  int BREAD = 63;
int   totalCalories;
```

The first statement named a constant, **BREAD**, and stored the value **63** into it. The second named a variable **totalCalories**, into which a value of type **int** can be stored.

We also said that variables and constants of integral and floating point types can be combined into expressions using arithmetic operators. The operations between constants or variables of these types are addition (+), subtraction (-), multiplication (*), and division (/). If the operands of the division operation are integral, the result is the integral quotient; if the operands are floating point types, the result is a floating point type with the division carried out to as many decimal places as the type allows. There is an additional operator for integral types, the modulus operator (%). This operator returns the remainder from integer division.

Precedence Rules

The precedence rules of arithmetic apply to arithmetic expressions in a program. That is, the order of execution of an expression containing more than one operation is determined by the precedence rules of arithmetic. These rules state that parentheses have the highest precedence; multiplication, division, and modulus have the next highest precedence; and addition and subtraction have the lowest. Because parentheses have the highest precedence, we can use them to change the order in which operations are executed.

Converting Numeric Types

If an integral and a floating point variable or constant are mixed in an operation, the integral value is changed temporarily to its equivalent floating point representation before the operation is executed. This automatic conversion of an integral value to a floating point value is called *type coercion*. Type coercion also occurs when a floating point value is assigned to an integral variable. Coercion from an integer to a floating point is exact. Although the two values are represented differently in memory, both representations are exact. However, when a floating point value is coerced into an integral value, loss of information occurs unless the floating point value is a whole number. That is, 1.0 can be coerced into 1, but what about 1.5? Is it coerced into 1 or 2? In C++ when a floating point value is coerced into an integral value, the floating point value is truncated. Thus, the floating point value 1.5 is coerced into 1.

Type changes can be made explicit by placing the value to be changed in parentheses and placing the name of the new type before it. That is,

```
intValue = 10.66;
```

and

```
intValue = int(10.66);
```

produce the same results. The first is implicit; the second is explicit. Explicit type changing is called *type casting* or *type conversion*, as opposed to implicit type changing, which is called *type coercion*. Explicit type conversion is more self-documenting and therefore is the better style.

Value-Returning Functions

Every C++ program must have an **int** function **main** that forms the main program. That is, **main** is the name of the function that calculates what we want the program to do (the action). We can also use functions to perform specific tasks within our function **main**. When we want the task to be executed, we use the function name in an expression.

C++ provides a wealth of preprogrammed function definitions to use. These function definitions are collected into files and made available through the

`#include` directive. For example, the `<math.h>` file provides access to such useful functions as `cos` and `sin` (which calculate the cosine and sine of a variable in radians), `pow` (which raises a value to a power), and `sqrt` (which takes the square root of a floating point value). These are all value-returning functions and are executed by using their names and arguments in an expression. Here is an example.

```
#include <math.h>
#include <iostream.h>

cout   << pow(3.0, 4.0)  << sqrt(81.0)  << endl;
```

`pow(3.0,  4.0)` returns the value `81.0`; this value is written on the screen. `sqrt(81.0)` returns the value `9.0`, which is also written on the screen. The values in the parentheses to the right of the function names are called *arguments* to the function. Arguments are the values that the functions use as input. In the case of `pow`, the first value is the one to be taken to a power and the second is the power. The parameter to `sqrt` is the value for which the square root is calculated.

You can write your own value-returning functions as well. Look at the following program.

```
// Program Miles prints miles in kilometers.

#include <iostream.h>

float  kilometers(int);

int main ()
{
    cout   << "One mile is " << kilometers(1)
           << " kilometers."  << endl;
    cout   << "Ten miles is " << kilometers(10)
           << " kilometers."  << endl;
    cout   << "One hundred miles is  << kilometers(100)
           << " kilometers."  << endl;
    return 0;
}

float  kilometers(int miles)
{
    const  KILO = 1.609;
    return KILO * float(miles);
}
```

Function `kilometers` is a user-defined, value-returning function. It takes one `int` parameter that represents miles and returns that value expressed in kilometers. Function `kilometers` is invoked by using its name in an output statement. That is, the value returned from the function is sent to the output stream. We discuss how to write value-returning functions in depth in Chapter 3.

Void Functions

C++ provides another type of function called a *void function*. A void function is the name of an action that does not return a single value. Value-returning functions like **main** have the data type of the value being returned before the name of the function (**int main**, for example). Void functions have the word **void** before the name of the function to indicate that they are not returning a single value. Rather than being used in an expression, void functions are used as statements in the body of other functions. We discuss void functions at great length in Chapter 3.

Output Formatting

We can control the vertical spacing of lines on the screen (or page) by using the **endl** manipulator. **endl** inserts an end-of-line character and forces the next output to begin on the next line. We can use successive **endl**'s to create blank lines. For example, the first of the following two statements creates three blank lines and writes the message "Happy New Year" on the fourth line.

```
cout  <<  endl  <<  endl  <<  endl  <<  "Happy New Year";
cout  <<  "!"
```

Where does the exclamation point go? Immediately following the *r* in *Year*. Characters are streamed to **cout** without line breaks unless **endl** is inserted into the stream.

We can put blanks in a line by including them within the strings that we are writing. For example, we can put extra blanks before and after the message as follows:

```
cout  <<  endl  <<  endl  <<  endl  <<     "  Happy New Year  ";
```

Note that we also added extra blanks before the double quote. These extra blanks have no effect on the output whatsoever. Only blanks within the strings are sent to **cout**.

When outputting numbers, it is useful to be able to state how many column positions the number should occupy. We can do so with another manipulator called setw. This manipulator (available in file <iomanip.h>) states how many columns the following data value is to occupy. For example,

```
intValue = 5;
cout  <<  setw(4)  <<  intValue;
```

prints the contents of **intValue** right-justified in four columns. The parameter to **setw** is an integer expression called the *fieldwidth*. If the fieldwidth is not large enough to contain the digits in the number, it is automatically expanded to the appropriate size. You specify the fieldwidth for floating point numbers the same way (don't forget to include the decimal point in your fieldwidth count). You can set the number of decimal places to be shown by the manipulator **setprecision** (also in file **<iomanip.h>**). For example,

```
realValue = 3.14159;
cout << setprecision(3) << realValue;
```

prints **3.142**.   Note that the last digit printed has been rounded.
setprecision(3) remains in effect until the next **setprecision** is used,
but **setw** applies only to the value immediately following.

Because the default spacing for floating point output may be different on
different systems, you can ensure that your floating point output looks the same by
including the following two statements in your program before sending any floating
point values to the output stream. Don't try to figure out what these statements
mean now; just use them.

```
cout.setf(ios::fixed, ios::floatfield);
cout.setf(ios::showpoint);
```

✓ Paper and Pencil Self Check #2

Examine the following program carefully and answer the question in Exercise 1.

```
Program Pres demonstrates the precedence of operators.

#include <iostream.h>

int main ()
{
    cout.setf(ios::fixed, ios::floatfield);
    cout.setf(ios::showpoint);
    cout << 4 + 3 * 5  << endl;
    cout << (4 + 3) * 5 <<endl;
    cout << 4 * 5 % 3 + 2  << endl;
    cout << (4 * (5 / 3) + 2)  << endl;
    return 0;
}
```

Exercise 1:   Show what is written by each of the output statements.

**Examine the following program carefully and then answer the questions in
Exercises 2 and 3 .**

```
// Program Format demonstrates the use of fieldwidth
// specifications.

#include <iostream.h>
#include <iomanip.h>
```

```
const int   INT_NUMBER = 1066;
const float  FLT_NUMBER = 3.14159;

main ()
{
    float  fltValue;
    int    intValue;

    cout.setf(ios::fixed, ios::floatfield);
    cout.setf(ios::showpoint);

    intValue = INT_NUMBER + FLT_NUMBER;
    fltValue = float(INT_NUMBER) + FLT_NUMBER;
    cout << INT_NUMBER  << endl;
    cout << intValue  << endl;
    cout << setw(10)  << intValue;
    cout << setw(10)  << intValue  << intValue /10  << endl;
    cout << setw(10)  << fltValue  << endl;
    cout << setprecision(10)  << fltValue  << endl
    cout << setw(10)  << setprecision(3)  << fltValue
         << endl;
    cout << fltValue << endl;
    cout << intValue  << setw(3)  << intValue  << setw(7)
         << intValue
         << endl;
    return 0;
}
```

Exercise 2:   Show what is written by each of the output statements.

Exercise 3:   Circle a statement that contains type conversion, and underline a statement that contains type coercion.

Program Input

Input Streams

There are four ways that a value can be stored in a place in memory. You have already seen two methods: a value can be stored by the compiler as the result of a constant declaration, or it can be stored as the result of an assignment statement. Here we introduce a third way: a value can be read into the program while the program is being executed. (We show you the fourth alternative in Chapter 3.)

In the last section, we said that **cout** was an output stream. Characters inserted into this stream appear on the screen. That is, the insertion operator (**<<**) inserts strings and values from within the program into the output stream that appears on the screen. In an analogous fashion, we can extract data values from an input stream prepared at the keyboard and store them in variables in our program. **cin** is the input stream from the keyboard, and **>>** is the extraction operator.

cout is of type **ostream**, and **cin** is of type **istream**. **istream**, **ostream**, **cin**, and **cout** are defined in file **<iostream.h>** and accessed by using the preprocessor directive **#include <iostream.h>**. Whereas statements using **cout** and the insertion operator (**<<**) place values in the output stream, statements using **cin** and the extraction operator (**>>**) take values from the input stream and place them in variables in the program.

The data type of the place in which a value is stored determines how the value is read. If you are reading numeric data, whitespace characters are skipped and an inappropriate character ends the input of the number. Whitespace characters are blanks and certain nonprintable characters, like the end-of-line character. If you are reading data into a variable of type **char**, whitespace characters are skipped and one character is read.

There are as many values read from the input stream as there are extraction operator/place name pairs to the right of **cin**. The values are extracted one at a time from the input stream and stored in the places named in order. The first value read goes into the first place listed, the second value read goes into the second place listed, etc. The values read must be of the same type as the places in which they are to be stored with the exception that a floating point value can be keyed as an integral value without a decimal point. The decimal point is automatically inserted in this case.

Because there are times when you do not want to skip whitespace before inputting a character, the **istream** data type provides a function to input the next character in the stream regardless of what it is. The function is named **get** and is applied as shown.

```
cin.get(character);
```

The next character in the input stream is returned in **char** variable **character**. If the previous input was a numeric value, **character** contains whatever inappropriate character ended the inputting of the value.

There are also times when you want to skip the rest of the values on a line and go to the beginning of the next line. There is a function called **ignore** defined in file **<iostream.h>** that lets you accomplish this task. It has two parameters. The first is an **int** expression and the second is a character. This function skips the number of characters specified in the first parameter or all the characters up to and including the character specified in the second parameter, whichever comes first. For example,

```
cin.ignore(80, '\n');
```

skips 80 characters or skips to the beginning of the next line depending on whether a newline character is encountered before 80 characters are skipped (read and discarded).

Keyboard Input Prompts

If your input is coming from the keyboard, someone is sitting at the keyboard waiting to enter the values at the proper time. The program should prompt the person to enter the values when it is ready to read them. For example, if the program needs the number of liters of paint purchased and the price of a liter, the person at the keyboard should be prompted with a message string something like this:

"Enter the number of liters of paint (whole number) followed by the cost of a liter (in Swedish kronor). Press return."

The statement that reads in the values follows the statement that writes the prompting message to the screen.

Files

If you want to prepare the input data ahead of time and store it on a file, or store output data on a file to use later, you may direct the program to read the data from a file or write data to a file by doing the following things:

1. Request the preprocessor to include file **<fstream.h>** as well as file **<iostream.h>**. The former contains the declarations for defining input and output streams other than cin and cout.
2. Declare an input stream to be of type ifstream or an output stream to be of type ofstream (or both).
3. Prepare the streams for use by using the function named **open** provided in file **<fstream.h>**. The parameter for function **open** is the external name of the file. The external name is the name under which the file is stored on the disk.
4. Put the file name to the left of the insertion or extraction operator.

Here is an example program that reads four floating point data values from a file and writes them to another file in reverse order.

```
// Program IODemo demonstrates how to use files.

#include <iostream.h>
#include <fstream.h>

int main()
{
    float val1, val2, val3, val4;   // declares 4 variables
    ifstream inData;                // declares input stream
    ofstream outData;               // declares output stream

    outData.setf(ios::fixed, ios::floatfield);
    outData.setf(ios::showpoint);

    inData.open("Data.In");
    // binds program variable inData to file "Data.In"

    outData.open("Data.Out");
    // binds program variable outData to file "Data.Out"

    inData  >> val1 >> val2 >> val3
            >> val4;                // inputs 4 values
    outData  << val4  << endl;
    outData  << val3  << endl;
    outData  << val2  << endl;
    outData  << val1  << endl;      // outputs 4 values
    return 0;
}
```

the operating system knows it by. Somehow these two names must be associated with one another. This association is called *binding* and is done in function `open`. Notice that `inData` and `outData` are identifiers declared in your program; `"Data.In"` and `"Data.Out"` are character strings. `Data.In` is the name that was used when the input data file was created; `Data.Out` is the name of the file where the answers are stored.

Input Failure

The key to reading data in correctly (from either the keyboard or a file) is to make sure that the order and the form in which the data are keyed are consistent with the order and type of the identifiers on the input stream extraction statement. If your data and your input statements are not consistent, your program does not crash or give an error message, but every subsequent stream operation is ignored. An error causes the stream to enter the fail state, and any further references to a stream in the fail state are ignored. If you misspell the name of the file that is the parameter to function `open` (`In.dat` instead of `Data.In`, for example), the stream enters the fail state. Your program continues to operate, but all references to `inData` are ignored.

Creating a Data File

If you are using an integrated environment, such as Turbo C++, in which an editor is provided for you to write your program, you may use the same editor to create a data file. That is, instead of writing a C++ program, you just key in the data you want the program to read.

If you are using a general-purpose word processor to create your programs, such as Word or WordPerfect, you need to save both your programs and your data files in text mode. General-purpose word processors have formatting information at the beginning of the file that you cannot see on the screen. This information must be removed from the file before the compiler can compile the program or the program can read data correctly. If the program file has formatting information, the compiler cannot compile the program and alerts you that there is a problem. If the data file has formatting information, you simply get the wrong answer.

✓ Paper and Pencil Self Check #3

Exercise 1: If file `Data.In` contains the values shown below, what does program `IODemo` write on file `Data.Out`?

```
5.5  6.6  7.7  8.8
```

Program `Frame` is an interactive program that reads the dimensions of a print and calculates the amount of wood needed to make a frame for it. Examine it carefully and then complete Exercises 2 through 6.

```
// Program Frame prompts the user to input values representing
// the dimensions of a print.  The amount of wood needed for
// the frame is calculated and printed on the screen.

#include <iostream.h>
```

```
int main ()
{
    int   side;              // vertical dimension in centimeters
    int   top;               // horizontal dimension in centimeters
    int   centimetersOfWood;    // centimeters of wood needed


    cout   << "Enter the vertical dimension of your print."
            << endl;
    cout   << "The dimension should be in whole centimeters. "
            << "Press return."  << endl;
    cin   >> side;

    cout   << "Enter the horizontal dimension of your print."
            << endl;
    cout   << "The dimension should be in whole centimeters. "
            << "Press return."  << endl;
    cin   >> top;

    centimetersOfWood = top + top + side + side;
    cout << "You need "   << centimetersOfWood
        <<" centimeters of wood."  << endl;
    return 0;
}
```

Exercise 2: Program Frame prompts for and reads the vertical dimension of the print and then prompts for and reads the horizontal dimension of the print. How many lines of input does program Frame expect? Explain.

What happens if you key both values at the same time with a blank between them?

Exercise 3: Hand-simulate program **Frame** with the following three sets of input values; record the value for **centimetersOfWood**.

top	*side*	*centimetersOfWood*
10	20	_____
13	5	_____
12	12	_____

Exercise 4: If the program is reorganized so that the prompts are together before the first input statement, what happens under the following reads? (The prompts are unchanged and the user follows them.)

a. cin >> side >> top;

b. cin >> side;
   cin >> top;

Exercise 5: What happens if you forget to put a space between the values for **side** and **top** in the input stream?

Exercise 6: Program **Frame** is to be changed to read from file **data**. Mark all the changes on program **Frame**.

_____

Chapter 1: Assignment Cover Sheet

Name _____ **Date**_____

Fill in the following table showing which exercises have been assigned for each lesson and check what you are to submit: (1) lab sheets, (2) listings of output files, and/or (3) listings of programs. Your instructor or TA can use the Completed column for grading purposes.

Activities	**Assigned:** Check or list exercise numbers	**Submit** (1) (2) (3)			**Completed**
Laboratory Exercises					
Lesson 1-1: C++ Syntax and Semantics, and the Program Development Process					
Lesson 1-2: Arithmetic Expressions, Function Calls, and Output					
Lesson 1-3: Program Input, and the Software Design Process					
Lesson 1-4: Debugging					
Programs from Scratch					

Lesson 1-1: C++ Syntax and Semantics, and the Program Development Process

Program Shell1 is the outline of a program. Use it for Exercise 1.

```
// Program Shell1

#include <iostream.h>

int main ()
{

    return 0;

}
```

Exercise 1: Add statements to program Shell1 to print the following information single spaced on the screen. Use literal constants in the output statements themselves for each of the data items to be written on the screen. Run your program to verify that the output is as specified.

a. your name (last name, comma, first name)
b. today's date (month:day:year)

Use program Shell2 for Exercises 2, 3, and 4.

```
// Program Shell2
#include <iostream.h>

const int   VALUE = 5;

int main ()
{
    int   intValue;

    cout << intValue;
    return 0;
}
```

Exercise 2: Add two assignment statements to program `Shell2`: one that stores `VALUE` into `intValue` and one that increments `intValue` by 1 using the plus operator (+). Run your program and record the results.

Exercise 3: Replace the plus operator in the program in Exercise 2 with the double plus operator and rerun your program. Are the results the same?

Exercise 4: Change the program in Exercise 2 so that it decrements `intValue` rather than incrementing it. You may use either the negative operator or the double negative operator. Record your results.

Lesson 1-2: Arithmetic Expressions, Function Calls, and Output

Use program `Convert` for Exercises 1 through 4. Study this program carefully. It converts a temperature from Fahrenheit to Celsius and a temperature from Celsius to Fahrenheit.

```
// Program Convert converts a temperature in Fahrenheit to
// Celsius and a temperature in Celsius to Fahrenheit.

#include <iostream.h>

const int TEMP_IN_F = 32;
const int TEMP_IN_C = 0;

int main ()
{
    int fToC;  // Place to store Celsius answer
    int cToF;  // Place to store the Fahrenheit answer

    cToF = (9 * TEMP_IN_C / 5) + 32;
    fToC = 5 * (TEMP_IN_F - 32) / 9;
    cout  << TEMP_IN_F  << " in Fahrenheit is "  << fToC
          << " in Celsius. "  << endl;
    cout  << TEMP_IN_C  << " in Celsius is "  << cToF
          << " in Fahrenheit. "  << endl;
    return 0;
}
```

Exercise 1: Compile and run program Convert. What values are written out for **fToC** and **cToF**?

Exercise 2: Change the values for constants **TEMP_IN_F** and **TEMP_IN_C** to the following values and compile and rerun the program after each change. Record the values for **fToC** and **cToF** for each set of values.

TEMP_IN_F	TEMP_IN_C	fToC	cToF
a. 212	100	_____	_____
b. 100	50	_____	_____
c. 122	37	_____	_____
d. ____	____	_____	_____

(You choose.)

Exercise 3: Examine the output from b and c. There seems to be an inconsistency. Describe the inconsistency and make a hypothesis to explain it.

Exercise 4:   Change the integer constants and variables to type **float** and rerun the program with the same data you used in parts b and c in Exercise 3. Do the results confirm your hypothesis?

Use the following shell for the next two exercises.

```
// Program Function demonstrates the use of library and
// user-defined functions.

#include <iostream.h>
#include <math.h>

float answer(float, float, float);

int main ()
{
    cout.setf(ios::fixed, ios::floatfield);
    cout.setf(ios::showpoint);

    cout  << answer(_____, _____, _____);
    return 0;
}

float answer(float one, float two, float three)
{
    return ((- two + sqrt(pow(two, _____)
        - (4.0 * one * three))) / (2.0 * one));
}
```

Exercise 5: Fill in the blanks in function **answer** such that the value stored in parameter **two** is taken to the second power. Fill in the blanks in function **main** so that function **answer** is invoked with **10.0** as the first parameter, **20.0** as the second parameter, and **5.0** as the third parameter. What is printed?

Exercise 6: Change the program in Exercise 5 so that function **answer** is invoked with **5.0** as the first parameter, **20.0** as the second parameter, and **10.0** as the third parameter. What is printed?

Exercise 7: Change the program in Exercise 6 so that function answer is invoked with **5.0** as the first parameter, **10.0** as the second parameter, and **20.0** as the third parameter. What happens?

Lesson 1-3: Program Input and the Software Design Process

Exercise 1: Program **InOut** reads values from the keyboard but does not give any prompts. Compile and execute this program. Enter the following values from the keyboard exactly as shown. *Do not look at the code.*

```
11   12   13   14
21   22
31   32
41
51
```

What values are printed?

a _____   b _____   c _____   d _____   e _____

f _____   g _____   h _____

This program contains five input-related statements. What must these statements be to give the results shown?

Use program CharRead for Exercise 2.

```cpp
// Program CharRead prompts for and reads four characters
// from the keyboard and then prints them.

#include <iostream.h>

int main ()
{
    char    char1;
    char    char2;
    char    char3;
    char    char4;
    cout  << "Input four characters.  Press Return."
          << endl;
    cin  >> char1  >> char2  >> char3  >> char4;
    cout  << char1  << char2  << char3  << char4;
    return 0;
}
```

Exercise 2:   Compile and run this program four times using the four sets of data values shown. Key these values exactly as shown, including blanks.

Input Data	*What Is Printed*
abcd	_____
a b c d	_____
1b2c	_____
31 45	_____

Examine the results carefully. Do any of the results surprise you? (Remember that the extraction operator skips whitespace.)

Exercise 3:   This exercise also reads character data.

```
// Program Char2Rd prompts for and reads four characters
// from the keyboard and then prints them.

#include <iostream.h>

int main ()
{
    char    char1;
    char    char2;
    char    char3;
    char    char4;

    cout  << "Input four characters.   Press Return."  << endl;
    cin.get(char1);
    cin.get(char2);
    cin.get(char3);
    cin.get(char4);
    cout  << char1  << char2  << char3  << char4;
    return 0;
}
```

Compile and run this program four times using the four sets of data values listed below. Key these values exactly as shown, including blanks.

Input Data	*What Is Printed*
abcd	_____
a b c d	_____
1b2c	_____
31 45	_____

Examine the results carefully. Do any of the results surprise you? (Remember that the function **get** does not skip whitespace.)

Program Frame4 gets its input from a file. Use it for Exercises 4 and 5

```
// Program Frame4 reads input values that represent the
// dimensions of a print from a file and calculates and
// prints the amount of wood needed for a frame.

#include <iostream.h>
#include <fstream.h>


int main ()
{
    ifstream  din;      // input stream
    int   side;         // vertical dimension in centimeters
    int   top;          // horizontal dimension in centimeters
    int   centimetersOfWood; // centimeters of wood needed

    din.open("Frame.In");
    din  >> side  >> top;
    cout  << "Dimensions are " << top  << " and "
          << side  << "."  << endl;
    centimetersOfWood = top + top + side + side;
    cout  << "You need "  << centimetersOfWood
          <<" centimeters of wood."  << endl;
    return 0;
}
```

Exercise 4: Create a data file on the same directory as program **Frame4**, and name it **Frame.In**. Make the values in the file consistent with the input statements. Run program **Frame4** and record the output below.

Exercise 5: Change program **Frame4** so that the output goes to file **dout**; **dout**'s external name should be **Frame.Out**. You must do the following tasks:
* Declare **dout** to be of type **ofstream**.
* Invoke function **open** to associate the internal name and the external name.
* Send the output to stream **dout**.
Run your changed program. Show what was written on file **Frame.Out**.

Lesson 1-4: Debugging

Exercise 1:   Program **Typos** contains syntax errors. Correct the program, describe the errors, and show what is printed. Then list the syntax errors, and show what is printed when the code compiles cleanly.

Exercise 2:   The output from program **Typos** looks strange! Clearly there are logic bugs lurking in the code. Find and correct these errors.

List the logic errors, and show what is printed when the logic errors are corrected.

Exercise 3.   Program **FourVals** reads four **int** values from a file and writes them out with exactly one blank between them.   The program doesn't even compile! List the syntax errors, correct them, and run the program. Show your output.

Exercise 4:   Now the program runs, but the output does not meet its specifications. Describe this logic error, correct it, and rerun the program. Show your output.

Exercise 5:   Run your program using file **Four2Val.in**. (You must edit the file name in the program.) Describe what happens.

Exercise 6: Program **FourVals** makes an assumption about the data that is not stated in the problem. What is this assumption?

How would you have to change program **FourVals** in order for it to work properly on file **Four2Val.in**?

Programs from Scratch

Exercise 1:   Write a program to print out the following lines from Dr. Seuss's *Horton Hatches the Egg*.[1]

I meant what I said
and I said what I meant
An elephant's faithful
one hundred percent

Put a border of asterisks around the entire quotation (all four sides). Each line of the quotation should be sent to the output stream in the same statement.

Exercise 2:   Write a program that produces a cover sheet for your laboratory assignments. It should have the chapter number, the lessons that have been assigned, your instructor's name, your name, the date, and any other information that your instructor has requested.

Exercise 3:   Write a program that converts a constant, **PENNIES**, to dollars and cents. Set the constant **PENNIES** to a value that is evenly divisible by 100, run your program, and show your output. Change the constant to a value that is not evenly divisible by 100, run your program, and show your output. Be sure to label your output appropriately.

Exercise 4:   Set **PENNIES** to zero and rerun your program. Write a paragraph describing what happens.

Exercise 5:   Write a program that prints the hundreds digit in a series of integer constants. For example, if constants **ONE** and **TWO** are **1456** and **254** respectively, your program should print 4 and 2. You may choose the integers yourself. Your output should include the original number followed by the digit in the hundreds position. Label your output appropriately.

Exercise 6:   Write a program that prints the number 1349.9431 with three decimal places, with two decimal places, and with one decimal place.

---

[1]Dr. Seuss, *Horton Hatches the Egg* (New York: Random House, 1940).

Conditions, Logical Expressions, and Control Structures

OBJECTIVES

- To be able to construct Boolean expressions to evaluate a given condition.
- To be able to construct If-Then statements to perform a specified task.
- To be able to construct If-Then-Else statements to perform a specified task.
- To be able to construct nested If statements to perform a specified task.
- To be able to design and implement a test plan.
- To be able to debug a program with a selection control structure.
- To be able to modify a program containing a While statement.
- To be able to construct a count-controlled loop to implement a specified task.
- To be able to construct an event-controlled loop to implement a specified task.
- To be able to construct a loop nested within another loop.
- To be able to test the state of an I/O stream.
- To be able to answer questions about a loop that you have implemented.
- To be able to convert a series of If-Then-Else statements to a Switch statement.
- To be able to construct a Switch statement to implement a specified task.
- To be able to convert a While loop to a Do-While loop.
- To be able to construct a Do-While loop to do a specified task.
- To be able to construct a For statement to do a specified task.

Conditions and Logical Expressions

The physical order of a program is the order in which the statements are *listed*. The logical order of a program is the order in which the statements are *executed*. In this chapter, you learn to ask questions in your program and change the order in which the statements are executed depending on the answer to your question.

Boolean Data Type

To ask a question in a program, you make a statement. If your statement is true, the answer to the question is yes. If your statement is not true, the answer to the question is no. You make these statements in the form of *Boolean expressions*. A Boolean expression asserts (states) that something is true. The assertion is evaluated and if it is true, the Boolean expression is true. If the assertion is not true, the Boolean expression is false.

Many programming languages have a data type Boolean with two values, *true* and *false*. The proposed C++ standard has such a type: **bool** (for Boolean) with constants **true** and **false**. If your compiler does not recognize **bool**, you can simulate the Boolean data type in C++ with the following declarations:

```
typedef int bool;
const bool  true = 1;
const bool  false = 0;
```

typedef is a statement that allows us to give a new name to an existing type. Here we are saying that **bool** is a new name for **int**. When the program is compiled, the word **int** is substituted for the word **bool** throughout the program. We have defined two constants, **true** and **false**, which are synonyms for one and zero, respectively. Now we can write our program using **true** and **false** rather than the integers one and zero.

Why do we go to all this trouble when one and zero work just fine? Because Boolean values are logically different from integer values. C++ encodes true as nonzero and false as zero, but conceptually the logical values true and false are not numbers. By using the constants **true** and **false** we make that distinction clear—both to ourselves and to anyone reading the program. From now on, we assume that type **bool** is defined, either as a built-in type or by including the declarations shown above.

Boolean Expressions

A Boolean expression can be a simple Boolean variable or constant or a more complex expression involving one or more of the relational operators. Relational operators take two operands and test for a relationship between them. Here are the relational operators and the C++ symbols that stand for them.

C++ Symbol Relationship

C++ Symbol	Relationship
= =	Equal to
! =	Not equal to

>	Greater than
<	Less than
> =	Greater than or equal to
< =	Less than or equal to

For example, the Boolean expression

```
number1 < number2
```

is evaluated to **true** if the value stored in **number1** is less than the value stored in **number2**, and evaluated to **false** otherwise.

When a relational operator is applied between variables of type **char**, the assertion is in terms of where the two operands fall in the collating sequence of a particular character set. For example,

```
character1 < character2
```

is evaluated to true if the character stored in **character1** comes before the character stored in **character2** in the collating sequence of the machine on which the expression is being evaluated. Although the collating sequence varies among machines, you can think of it as being in alphabetic order. That is, *A* always comes before *B* and *a* always before *b*, but the relationship of *A* to *a* may vary.

We must be careful when applying the relational operators to floating point operands, particularly equal (==) and not equal (!=). Integer values can be represented exactly; floating point values with fractional parts often are not exact in the low-order decimal places. Therefore, you should compare floating point values for near equality. For example if you only want to see if two floating point values are the same within .001, you could use the following test:

```
if (value1 - value2 < 0.001)
```

A simple Boolean expression is either a Boolean variable or constant or an expression involving the relational operators that evaluates to either true or false. These simple Boolean expressions can be combined using the logical operations defined on Boolean values. There are three Boolean operators: AND, OR, and NOT. Here is a table showing the meaning of these operators and the symbols that are used to represent them in C++.

C++ Symbol   *Meaning*

& &	AND is a binary Boolean operator. If both operands are true, the result is true. Otherwise, the result is false.
| |	OR is a binary Boolean operator. If at least one of the operands is true, the result is true. Otherwise, the result is false.

!	NOT is a unary Boolean operator. NOT changes the value of its operand: if the operand is true, the result is false; if the operand is false, the result is true.

If both relational operators and Boolean operators are combined in the same expression in C++, the Boolean operator NOT (!) has the highest precedence, the relational operators have next higher precedence, and the Boolean operators AND (&&) and OR (||) come last (in that order). Expressions in parentheses are always evaluated first.

For example, given the following expression (**stop** is a **bool** variable)

```
count <= 10 && sum >= limit || !stop
```

!stop is evaluated first, the expressions involving the relational operators are evaluated next, the **&&** is applied, and finally the **||** is applied. C++ uses *short-circuit evaluation*. The evaluation is done in left-to-right order and halts as soon as the result is known. For example, in the above expression if both of the arithmetic expressions are true, the evaluation stops because the left operand to the OR operation (**||** operator) is true. There is no reason to evaluate the rest of the expression: true **||** anything is true.

The precedence of all the operators we have seen so far is summarized in the following table.

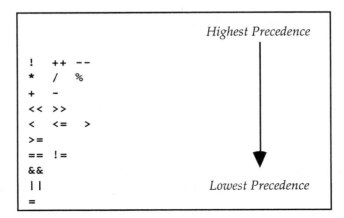

If-Then and If-Then-Else Statements

The If statement allows the programmer to change the logical order of a program; that is, make the order in which the statements are executed differ from the order in which they are listed in the program.

The If-Then statement uses a Boolean expression to determine whether to execute a statement or to skip it.

```
if (number < 0)
    number = 0;
sum = sum + number;
```

The expression (**number** < 0) is evaluated. If the result is true, the statement **number** = 0 is executed. If the result is false, the statement is skipped. In either case, the next statement to be executed is **sum** = **sum** + **number**. The statement that is either executed or skipped may be a *block*. A block is a group of statements in the action part of the program enclosed in braces.

The If-Then-Else statement uses a Boolean expression to determine which of two statements to execute.

```
cout << "Today is a ";
if (temperature <= 5)
    cout << "cold ";
else
    cout << "nice ";
cout << "day." << end
```

The characters "**Today is a** " are sent to the output stream. The expression (**temperature** <= 5) is evaluated. If the result is true, the characters "**cold** " are sent to the output stream. If the result is false, the characters "**nice** " are sent to the output stream. In either case, the next statement to be executed sends the characters "**day.**" to the output stream. Either of the statements may be a block (compound statement) as shown in the following example.

```
if (temperature <= 5)
{
    cout << "Today is a cold day." << endl;
    cout << "Sitting by the fire is appropriate." << endl;

}
else
{
    cout << "Today is a nice day." << endl;
    cout << "How about taking a walk?" << endl;
}
```

There is a point of C++ syntax that you should note: you do not need a semicolon after the right brace of a block (compound statement) in the executable part of the program.

Nested Logic

An If-Then statement uses a Boolean expression to determine whether to execute a statement or skip it. An If-Then-Else statement uses a Boolean expression to determine which of two statements to execute. The statements to be executed or skipped can be simple statements or blocks (compound statements). There is no constraint on what the statements can be. This means that the statement to be skipped in an If-Then statement can be another If statement. In the If-Then-Else statement, either or both of the choices can be another If statement. An If statement within another If statement is called a *nested* If statement.

The following is an example of a nested If statement.

```
cout << "Today is a ";
```

```
if (temperature <= 5)
    cout << "cold ";
else if (temperature <= 20)
    cout << "nice ";
else
    cout << "hot ";
cout << "day." << endl;
```

Notice that the nested If statement does not have to ask if the temperature is greater than 5 because we do not execute the **else** branch of the first If statement if the temperature is less than or equal to 5.

In nested If statements, there may be confusion over which **if** an **else** belongs. In the absence of braces, the compiler pairs an **else** with the most recent **if** that doesn't have an **else**. You can override this pairing by enclosing the preceding **if** in braces to make the **then** clause of the outer If statement complete.

State of an I/O Stream

In Chapter 1, we said that all references to an input or output stream are ignored if the stream is in the fail state. The fail state is entered if the file that is the parameter to the **open** operation isn't found, if you try to input from a stream after all the values have been read, or if invalid data is encountered in the input stream. C++ provides a way to test the state of a stream: the stream name used in an expression returns true if the state is okay and false if the stream is in the fail state. Look at the following example.

```
// Program Area demonstrates stream testing.
#include <iostream.h>
#include <fstream.h>

int main()
{
    int side1;      // one side of a rectangle
    int side2;      // the other side of a rectangle
    ifstream inData; // file stream
    int area;       // area of rectangle

    inData.open("myData.dat");
    if (!inData)
    {
        cout  << "Input file not found." << endl;
        return 1;
    }
    inData  >> side1  >> side2;
    if (!inData)
    {
        cout  << "Data format incorrect.";
        return 2;
    }
    area = side1 * side2;
    cout  << "Area is "  << area  << endl;
    return 0;
}
```

If the input file **myData.dat** cannot be found, **1** is returned to the operating system. If the data format on file **inData** is incorrect, **2** is returned to the operating system. If there are no input errors, **0** is returned to the operating system. Notice that the function **main** is exited as soon as a value is returned. Therefore, there are three ways that this function can be completed: two with an error (return **1** or **2**) and one with no error (return **0**). Returning **0** means normal completion of a program; returning any other value signals an error. When you are writing your program, you may choose the values to return to indicate different error conditions.

If a stream error occurs and you do not want the program to halt, you can use the function **clear** to reset the state of the stream. The following code segment resets the stream state and reads past the bad data.

```
cin.clear();
cin.ignore(5, '\n');
```

Test Plans

How do you test a specific program to determine its correctness? You design and implement a *test plan*. A test plan for a program is a document that specifies the test cases that should be run, the reason for each test case, and the expected output from each case. The test cases should be chosen carefully. The *code-coverage* approach designs test cases to ensure that each statement in the program is executed. The *data-coverage* approach designs test cases to ensure that the limits of the allowable data are covered. Often testing is a combination of code and data coverage.

Implementing a test plan means that you run each of the test cases described in the test plan and record the results. If the results are not as expected, you must go back to your top-down design and find and correct the error(s). The process stops when each of the test cases gives the expected results. Note that an implemented test plan gives you a measure of confidence that your program is correct; however, all you know for sure is that your program works correctly on your test cases. Therefore the quality of your test cases is extremely important.

An example of a test plan for the code fragment that tests temperatures is shown on the next page. We assume that the fragment is embedded in a program that reads in a data value that represents a temperature.

Reason for Test Case	Input Values	Expected Output	Observed Output
Test first end point	5	Today is a cold day.	
Test second end point	20	Today is a nice day.	
Test value below first end point	4	Today is a cold day.	
Test value between end points	15	Today is a nice day.	
Test value above second end point	21	Today is a hot day.	
Test negative value	-10	Today is a cold day.	

To implement this test plan, the program is run six times, once for each test case. The results are written in the Observed Output column.

Warning

The assignment operator (=) and the equality test operator (==) easily can be miskeyed one for the other. What happens if this occurs? Unfortunately, the program does not crash; it continues to execute but probably gives incorrect results. Look at the following two statements.

```
aValue == aValue + 1;     // aValue = aValue + 1 is meant

if (value1 = value2)      // if (value1 == value2) is meant
```

The first statement returns false: **aValue** can never be equal to **aValue + 1**. The semicolon ends the statement, so nothing happens to the value returned (**aValue + 1**) and execution continues with the next statement. **aValue** has not been changed. In the second case, although we think of **value1 = value2** as being an assignment statement, it is technically just an expression that does two things: it returns the value of the expression on the right of the equal sign, and it stores this value in the place on the left. Here, the value returned is the content of **value2**. If this value is not zero, true is returned; if **value2** contains zero, false is returned. We have more to say about the assignment statement actually being an expression in Chapter 4.

If one of the values in a test for equality is a constant (either named or literal), put it on the left-hand side of the operator. This way, if you miskey the assignment operator for the equality operator, the compiler catches the error.

The moral of this story is to be very careful when you key your program. A simple keying error can cause logic errors that the compiler does not catch and that are very difficult for the user to find. Great care and a good test plan are essential to C++ programming.

✓   ## Paper and Pencil Self Check #1

Examine program Convert and answer the questions in Exercises 1 through 3.

```
// Program Convert converts a temperature from Fahrenheit to
// Celsius or a temperature from Celsius to Fahrenheit
// depending on whether the user enters an F or a C.

#include <iostream.h>

int main ()
{
    char letter;          // Place to store input letter
    int tempIn;           // Temperature to be converted
    int tempOut;          // Converted temperature

    cout  <<"Input Menu" << endl  << endl;
    cout  <<"F:  Convert from Fahrenheit to Celsius"  << endl;
    cout  <<"C:  Convert from Celsius to Fahrenheit"  << endl;
    cout  <<"Type a C or an F, then press return."  << endl;
    cout  <<"Type an integer number, then press return."
          << endl;
```

```
cin  >> letter;
cin  >> tempIn;

if (letter == 'C')
    tempOut = (9 * tempIn / 5) + 32;
else
    tempOut = 5 * (tempIn - 32) / 9;
cout  << "Temperature to convert: "   << tempIn  << endl;
cout  << "Converted temperature:  "   << tempOut << endl;

return 0;
}
```

Exercise 1:   If the letter C and the value 100 are input, what is the output?

Exercise 2:   If the letter *F* and the value 32 are input, what is the output?

Exercise 3:   If the letter *c* and the value 0 are input, what is the output?

Exercise 4:   Examine the following pairs of expressions and determine if they are equivalent. Put a T in the Result column if they are the same and an F if they are not.

Expression 1	*Expression 2*	*Result*
!(A == B)	A != B	_____
!((A == B) || (A == C))	(A != B) && (A != C)	_____
!((A == B) && (C > D))	(A != B) || (C <= D)	_____

Exercise 5: Examine the following pairs of expressions and determine if they are equivalent. Put a T in the Result column if they are the same and an F if they are not.

Expression 1	*Expression 2*	*Result*
!A && B	B && !A	_____
!A || B	B || !A	_____
!(A && B)	A || B	_____
A && B || C	A && (B || C)	_____
(A && B || C)	!(A || B && C)	_____

Looping with the While Statement

Boolean expressions can be used in the If statement to make a choice. Boolean expressions can be used in a While statement to make the program repeat a statement or group of statements. Such repetitions are called *loops*.

While Statement

The If statement allows the program to skip the execution of a statement or choose between one of two statements to be executed based on the value of a Boolean expression. In contrast, the While statement allows a program to continue executing a statement as long as the value of a Boolean expression is true. When the Boolean expression becomes false, execution of the program continues with the statement immediately following the While statement. Look at the following code fragment.

```
sum = 0;
count = 1;
while (count <= 10)
{
    cin >> value;
    sum = sum + value;
    count++;
}
cout << "The sum of the 10 numbers is " << sum;
```

The variables **sum** and **count** are assigned the values **0** and **1** respectively. The Boolean expression (**count** **<=** **10**) is evaluated. The value in **count** is less than or equal to 10, so the expression is true and the block (compound statement) associated with the While is executed. A number is extracted from the standard input stream and added to **sum**. The value in **count** is incremented by 1.

At this point, the logical order of the program diverges from the physical order. The While expression is evaluated again. Because the value stored in **count** is still less than or equal to 10, the compound statement associated with the While is executed again. This process continues until **count** contains the value 11. At that time, the expression is no longer true, the body of the While statement is not executed again, and execution continues with the statement immediately following the While statement that sends the labeled answer to the output stream.

Types of Loops

There are two basic types of loops: count-controlled and event-controlled. A *count-controlled loop* is one that is executed a certain number of times. The expression that controls the loop becomes false when the loop has executed the prescribed number of times. An *event-controlled loop* is one whose execution is controlled by the occurrence of an event within the loop itself. The previous example is a count-controlled loop that executes 10 times. Let's look at an example of an event-controlled loop that reads and sums values from **cin** until a negative value is encountered.

```
bool  moreData;

sum = 0;

cin  >> value;

// Set moreData to true if the first data item is not
// negative; false otherwise.
moreData = value >= 0;

while (moreData)
{
    sum = sum + value;
    cin  >> value;
    moreData = value >= 0; // Reset moreData
}
cout  << "The sum of the values prior to a negative value is "
      << sum  << endl;
```

sum is set to zero and the first data item (**value**) is read outside of the loop. **value** is compared to zero and the result is stored in **moreData**. If the first data item is less than zero, **moreData** is **false**, and the body of the loop is not executed. If the first data item is greater than or equal to zero, **moreData** is true, and the body of the loop is entered. **value** is added to **sum**, and the next data item is read. This new data item is compared to zero, and **moreData** is reset. The expression is tested again. This process continues until a value of less than zero is read and **moreData** becomes false. When this happens, the body of the While is not executed again, and the sum of the nonnegative numbers is sent to the output stream.

Reading the first value outside of the body of the loop is called a priming read. When a priming read is used before a loop, the input values are processed at the beginning of the loop body and a subsequent read occurs at the end of the loop body.

Notice the difference between these two loops. The first reads ten values and sums them; the second reads and sums values until a negative number if read. The first is count-controlled; the second is event-controlled. The second loop is called a sentinel-controlled loop because reading a sentinel (a negative number) is the event that controls it.

EOF Loops

In Chapter 1, we stated that running out of data puts the input stream into the fail state. We also said that the stream name can be used to test to see if the stream is in the fail state. We can put these two facts together to construct a very useful event-controlled loop for reading data values. We can read and process data values until the stream goes into the fail state. When the last data value has been read, the stream is at the end of the file (called EOF). The stream is fine until another data value is requested. At that point, the stream goes into the fail state. This means that we must try to read one more value than exists on the stream in order to let the fail state control the reading. The following loop reads and sums values until there is no more data.

```
sum = 0;
cin >> value;
```

```
while (cin)
{
    sum = sum + value;
    cin >> value;
}
```

Because **cin** does not go into the fail state until we try to access a value when the stream is at EOF, we must use a priming read as we did in the previous example. If there is a value, (**cin**) returns true and the body of the loop is entered where the value is added to **sum** and a new value is read. After the last value has been processed, the attempt to read one more value causes **cin** to enter the fail state. When the While expression is tested the last time, (**cin**) returns false and the loop is not repeated.

Proper Loop Operation

For obvious reasons, the While statement is called a loop or looping statement. The statement that is being executed within the loop is called the *body* of the loop.

There are three basic steps that must be completed for a loop to operate properly.

1. The variables in the expression (the counter or event) must be set (initialized) before the While statement is executed the first time.
2. The expression must test the status of the counter or event correctly so that the body of the loop executes when it is supposed to and terminates at the proper time.
3. The counter or the event must be updated within the loop. If the counter or the event is not updated, the loop never stops executing. This situation is called an infinite loop.

Nested Loops

The body of the loop can contain any type of statement including another While statement. The following program counts the number of characters on each line in a file. We know that the manipulator **endl** forces the next characters sent to the output stream to begin a new line. How can we recognize a new line on the input stream? A new line begins following the symbol '**\n**'. We must be sure to use function **get** defined in file **<iostream.h>**, not the extraction operator, to input each character.

```
// Program LineCt counts the number of characters per line
// and the number of lines in a file.
// There is a '\n' before the EOF.

#include <iostream.h>
#include <fstream.h>
int main()
{
    int  lineNo;
    char character;
    int  number;
    fstream inData;
```

```
inData.open("Data.In");
lineNo = 0;
inData.get(character);
while (inData)
{
    lineNo++;
    number = 0;
    while (character != '\n')
    {
        number++;
        inData.get(character);
    }
    cout  << "Line "  << lineNo  << " contains "
          << number  << " characters."  << endl;
    inData.get(character);
}
return 0;
}
```

✓ Paper and Pencil Self Check #2

Read program **Count** carefully.

```
// Program Count prompts for, reads, echo prints, and sums a
// fixed number of integer values.  The sum is printed.
#include <iostream.h>

const int  LIMIT = 10;

int main ()
{
    int   counter;                // loop-control variable
    int   sum;                    // summing variable
    int   dataValue;              // input value
    counter = 1;
    sum = 0;

    // Input and sum integer data values.
    while (counter <= LIMIT)
    {
        cout  << "Enter an integer value.  Press return."
              << endl;
        cin  >> dataValue;
        sum = sum + dataValue;
        counter++;
    }
    cout  << "Sum is "  << sum  << endl;
    return 0;
}
```

Exercise 1:   What is printed, if the following data values are entered as prompted?

8   5   3   -2   0   9   1   7   3   10

Exercise 2: Is the loop in program `Count` a count-controlled loop or an event-controlled loop? Explain.

Read program `Count2` carefully.

```
// Program Count2 prompts for, reads, and sums integer
// values until a negative number is read.  The input
// values and the sum are printed.

#include <iostream.h>

int main ()
{
    int  sum;        // summing variable
    int  dataValue;  // input value
    sum = 0;
    cout  << "To stop processing, enter a negative"
          << " value."  << endl;
    cout  << " Enter an integer value; press return."
          << endl;
    // Read first data value to prepare for loop.
    cin  >> dataValue;

    // Input and sum integer data values
    while (dataValue > 0)
    {
        sum = sum + dataValue;
        cout  << "Enter an integer value; press return."
              << endl;
        cin  >> dataValue;
    }
    cout  << "Sum is "  << sum  << endl;
    return 0;
}
```

Exercise 3: What is printed, if the following data values are entered one per line?

   8   5   3   -2   0   9   1   7   3   10

Exercise 4: Is the loop in program `Count2` a count-controlled loop or an event-controlled loop? Explain.

Additional Control Structures

We have covered three control structures: the sequence, the If statement, and the While statement. In this section, we introduce five additional control structures that make certain tasks easier. However, they are the icing on the cake. You cannot do anything with them that you cannot do with the control structures that you already know .

Break and Continue

Both **break** and **continue** are statements that alter the flow of execution within a control structure. **break** is used with the Switch statement, the While statement, the Do-While statement, and the For statement. (The Switch, Do-While, and For statements are defined below.) **break** interrupts the flow of control by immediately exiting these statements. In contrast, **continue** is used only with looping statements. It alters the flow of control by immediately terminating the current iteration. Note the difference between **continue** and **break** in a loop: **continue** skips to the next iteration of the loop, and **break** skips to the statement following the loop.

    break is extremely useful with the Switch statement but should be used cautiously with looping statements. Good style dictates that loops have only one entry and one exit except under very unusual circumstances. **continue** is very seldom used; we only mention it for completeness.

Multi-Way Branching: Switch

The *Switch* statement is a selection statement that can be used in place of a series of If-Then-Else statements. Alternative statements are listed with a *switch label* in front of each. A switch label is either a *case label* or the word **default**. A case label is the word **case** followed by a constant expression. An integral expression called the *switch expression* is used to match one of the values on the case labels. The statement associated with the value that is matched is the statement that is executed. Execution then continues sequentially from the matched label until the end of the Switch statement or a Break statement is encountered.

```
switch (grade)
{
    case 'A' : cout  << "Great work!";
               break;
    case 'B' : cout  << "Good work!";
               break;
    case 'C' : cout  << "Passing work!";
               break;
    case 'D' :
    case 'F' : cout  << "Unsatisfactory work.";
               cout  << "See your instructor.";
               break;
    default  : cout  << grade  << " is not a legal grade";
               break;
}
```

`grade` is the switch expression; the letters beside the statements make up the case labels. The value in `grade` is compared with the value in each case label. When a match is found, the corresponding statement is executed. If the value of the switch expression does not match a value in any case label, the `default` label is matched by default. Because execution continues after a match until `break` is encountered, both 'D' and 'F' send the same message to the screen. What would happen if we forgot to put `break` after the statement associated with `case 'B'`? Every time `grade` contained a *B* both "Good work!" and "Passing work!" would be printed.

Looping: Do-While

The *Do-While* statement is a looping statement that tests the Boolean expression at the end of the loop. A statement (or sequence of statements) is executed while an expression is true. The Do-While statement differs from the While statement in one major respect: the body of the loop is always executed at least once in the Do-While statement. For example, the following loop reads and counts characters in stream `inFile` until a blank is found.

```
numberOfCharacters = 0;
inFile  >> character;

// assume first character is not a blank
do
{
    numberOfCharacters++;
    inFile >> character;
} (while character != ' ');
```

We may use the Do-While statement to construct both count-controlled and event-controlled loops.

Looping: For

In contrast, the *For* statement is a looping construct designed specifically to simplify the implementation of count-controlled loops. The loop-control variable, the beginning value, the ending value, and the incrementation are explicitly part of the For heading itself. The following For loop reads and sums 10 values.

```
sum = 0;
for (counter = 1; counter <= 10; counter++)
{
    cin  >> value;
    sum = sum + value;
}
```

`counter`, the loop-control variable, is initialized to 1. While `counter` is less than or equal to 10, the block of code is executed, and `counter` is incremented by 1. The loop is executed with `counter` equal to the initial value, the final value, and all the values in between. The second expression in the For heading is the assertion that controls the loop. If the assertion is false initially, the body of the loop is not executed. Here are two For headings and what they mean.

for (counter = limit; counter != 0; counter--):
Initialize `counter` to the value stored in `limit`; if `counter` is not equal
to 0, execute the body of the loop; decrement `counter` by 1 and go back to the
test. If `limit` contains the value 10, this For loop is identical to the previous
one: it executes 10 times.

for (int counter = 1; counter <= limit; counter++):
Define an `int` variable `counter` and initialize it to 1. If `counter` is less
than or equal to the value stored in `limit`, execute the body of the loop.
Increment `counter` by 1. The scope of `counter` is not the body of the loop
but the block in which the For statement is enclosed.

The For statement in C++ is very flexible. Although designed to simplify
count-controlled loops, it can be used for event-controlled loops. The first
statement in the For header can be any statement—even a stream extraction or the
null statement. The second statement is a test that occurs at the beginning of the
loop. The third statement is one that is executed at the end of the loop. So the For
heading

```
for (cin >> character; character != '.'; cin >> character)
```

is legal. In fact, no loop body (except the null statement—a semicolon) is needed
here because everything is done in the heading. However, we recommend that the
For statement be used only for count-controlled loops. That is what For statements
are designed for. Most other uses fall into the category of tricky code and should be
avoided. (How long did it take you to determine what this loop is doing?)

Loops constructed with the While statement and the For statement are called
pretest loops because the expression is tested at the beginning of the loop before
the body of the loop is executed the first time. Loops constructed with the Do-
While statement are called posttest loops because the expression is tested at the
end of the loop.

✓   ## Paper and Pencil Self Check #3

Read program Loops carefully and answer Exercises 1 and 2.

```
// Program Loops demonstrates various looping structures.
#include <iostream.h>
#include <fstream.h>
int main ()
{
    ifstream   inData;
    int   value;
    inData.open("Loop.dat");
// while loop
    {
        int   counter = 1;
        int   sum = 0;
        while (counter <= 4)
        {
            inData  >> value;
            sum = sum + value;
            counter++;
        }
```

```
            cout   << sum  << endl;
    }

// do-while loop
    {
        int   counter = 1;
        int   sum = 0;
        do
        {
            inData  >> value;
            sum = sum + value;
            counter++;
        } while (counter <= 4);
        cout   << sum  << endl;
    }

// for loop
    {
        int   sum = 0;
        for (int counter = 1; counter <= 4; counter++)
        {
            inData  >> value;
            sum = sum + value;
        }
        cout   << sum  << endl;
    }
    return 0;
}
```

Exercise 1: If file **Loops.dat** contains the following values, what is printed?

```
10 20 30 40 10 20 30 40 10 20 30 40
```

Exercise 2: Which of these loops are pretest loops? Which are posttest?

Examine program Switches and answer Exercises 3 and 4.

```
// Program Switches demonstrates the use of the Switch
// statement.
#include <iostream.h>

int main ()
{
    char   letter;
    int    first;
    int    second;
    int    answer;
```

```
            cout  << "Enter an A for addition or an S for"
                  << " subtraction, followed by two integer "
                  << endl
                  << " numbers.  Press return.  Enter a Q to quit."
                  << endl;
        cin  >> letter;
        while (letter != 'Q')
        {
            cin  >> first  >> second;
          switch (letter)
          {
              case 'A' : answer = (first + second);
                         cout << first  << " + "  << second
                                << " is "  << answer  << endl;
                         break;
              case 'S' : answer = (first - second);
                         cout << first  << " - "  << second
                                << " is "   << answer  << endl;
                         break;
          }
            cin  >> letter;
        }
        return 0;
}
```

Exercise 3:   What is printed if the following values are entered?

```
A   5   -7
A  -5   -8
S   7    7
S   8   -8
Q
```

Exercise 4:   What happens if the Q to quit is entered as a lower case letter?

Chapter 2: Assignment Cover Sheet

Name _____ **Date** _____

Fill in the following table showing which exercises have been assigned for each lesson and check what you are to submit: (1) lab sheets, (2) listings of output files, and/or (3) listings of programs. Your instructor or TA can use the Completed column for grading purposes.

Activities	Assigned: Check or list exercise numbers	Submit (1) (2) (3)			Completed
Laboratory Exercises					
Lesson 2-1: If-Then and If-Then-Else Statements					
Lesson 2-2: Looping with the While Statement					
Lesson 2-3: Additional Control Structures					
Lesson 2-4: Test Plan					
Lesson 2-5: Debugging					
Programs from Scratch					

Lesson 2-1: If-then and If-then-Else Statements

Use program **Shell1** for Exercises 1, 2, and 3. This program prompts for and reads an integer value, and then prints a message based on this value.

```
// Program Shell1 prints appropriate messages based on a
// pressure reading input from the keyboard.

#include <iostream.h>

main ()
{
    int count;
    int pressure;

    for (count = 1; count <= 8; count++)
    {
        cout << "Enter an integer pressure reading. "
             << " Press Return."  << endl;
        cin >> pressure;
        /* FILL IN Code appropriate to exercise */
    }
    return 0;
}
```

Exercise 1:   Insert a statement that writes the following warning to the screen if the pressure reading is greater than 100.

"Warning!! Pressure reading above danger limit."

Run your program using the following values as input: 5, 75, 80, 99, 0, 100, 110, 199.

"Warning !! Pressure reading above danger limit." is printed _____ times.

If your answer is 2, your If statement is correct. If your answer is 3, the relational operator on your expression is incorrect. It should be greater than, not greater than or equal to. Rerun your corrected program.

Exercise 2:   Insert a statement in program **Shell1** that writes the following message if the pressure reading is lower than 100 but greater than 5.

"Everything seems normal."

Run your program using the same data that you used in Exercise 1.

"Everything seems normal" is printed _____ times.

Exercise 3:   Take program **Shell1** in Exercise 2 and change it so that it prints the message in both Exercise 1 and Exercise 2. Run the program with the data set for Exercise 1.

"Warning !! Pressure reading above danger limit." is printed _____ times.

"Everything seems normal" is printed _____ times.

Use the following shell for the Exercises 4 and 5.

```
// Program Shell2 reads in a temperature and prints an
// appropriate message.

#include <iostream.h>

int main ()
{
    int   count;
    int   temperature;

    for (count = 1; count <= 5; count++)
    {
        cout  << "Enter the temperature in your room."
              << endl;
        cin  >> temperature;

        /* TO BE FILLED IN */
    }
    return 0;
}
```

Exercise 4:   Add five If-Then statements to program **Shell2** so that one of the following messages is printed based on the value of **temperature**.

Temperature	Message
> 30	"Visit a neighbor."
<= 30, > 22	"Turn on air conditioning."
<= 22, > 19	"Do nothing."
<= 19, >12	"Turn on heat."
<= 12	"Visit a neighbor."

Run your program with data values so that each message is written exactly once. What data values did you use?

Exercise 5:   Rewrite the program in Exercise 4 using nested logic (that is, If-Then-Else where the Else branch is an If statement). Rerun the program with the same data. Did you get the same answers? If you didn't, you have an error.

Exercise 6:   Complete program **HiScore** so that it reads and prints three test scores, then labels and prints the largest of the three.

```
// Program HiScore reads and prints three test scores.
// The largest value of the three is printed with an
// appropriate message.
// Assumption:  The scores are unique.

#include <iostream.h>

int main ()
{
    int   test1Score;
    int   test2Score;
    int   test3Score;

    cout  << "Enter score for test 1; press return."  << endl;
    cin   >> test1Score;
    cout  << "Enter score for test 2; press return."  << endl;
    cin   >> test2Score;
    cout  << "Enter score for test 3; press return."  << endl;
    cin   >> test3Score;

    cout  << "The three test scores are: "  << endl;
    cout  << test1Score  << endl;
    cout  << test2Score  << endl;
    cout  << test3Score  << endl;

    /* TO BE FILLED IN */
    return 0;
}
```

Fill in the missing statement(s) in program **HiScore** so that the largest of the
three input values (scores) is printed and labeled as the highest test score. You
may use a nested If statement or a series of If statements.   For example, if
test2Score with a value of 98 is the largest, your output might look as
follows:

```
The value for test 2 is the highest; it is 98.
```

Your message may be different, but it must include the largest value and which test
had that value. Run your program three times using the three sets of input values
listed below.

Input values			*What Is printed*
100	80	70	_____
70	80	100	_____
80	100	60	_____

Lesson 2-2: Looping with the While Statement

Exercise 1: Change program `Count` in the Pencil and Paper Self Check so that the number of values to be read (`limit`) is input from the keyboard rather than being set as a named constant. Run your program using a value of 10 and enter the same data:

```
9   5   3   -2   0   9   1   7   3   10
```

(Don't forget to prompt for `limit`.) Your answer should be the same. If it is not, you have an error.

Exercise 2: Run program `Count` entering one fewer data value than called for. What happens?

Exercise 3: Run program `Count` entering one more data value than called for. What happens?

Exercise 4: Examine program `Shell3`. When completed, program `Shell3` prompts for and reads a one-digit number, then adds the numbers from zero to the number, inclusive, and prints the sum.

```cpp
// Program Shell3 prompts for and reads a one-digit number.
// Values between 0 and the digit (inclusive) are summed.

#include <iostream.h>

int main ()
{
    int   counter;    // loop-control variable
    int   sum;        // running sum
    int   digit;

    cout  << "Enter a one-digit number; press return."
          << endl;
    cin  >> digit;
    counter =  /* TO BE FILLED IN */
    sum   =    /* TO BE FILLED IN */

    while /* TO BE FILLED IN  */
    {
      /*  TO BE FILLED IN */
    }
    cout  << "Sum of digits between 0 and "
          << digit  << " is "  << sum  << endl;
    return 0;
}
```

Fill in the appropriate initializations and the body of the While loop so that the sum of the digits from zero through `digit` (the input value) is computed. Run your program four times using 0, 3, 7, and 9 as the input values.

Answer for 0:   _____   Answer for 3:   _____

Answer for 7:   _____   Answer for 9:   _____

Exercise 5:   Rewrite your solution to the previous exercise so that the processing is repeated until a negative digit is read. That is, embed your solution within another loop that continues to prompt for a digit and calculates the sum of the digits from zero through `digit` as long as `digit` is positive. The process stops when `digit` is negative. Be sure to add this information to the prompt. Rewrite the program documentation at the beginning of the program to reflect this change. Run your program once using the same data.

What additional documentation did you include?

Is the outer loop a count-controlled loop or an event-controlled loop?

Use Shell4 for Exercises 6 and 7.

```
// Program Shell4 prints appropriate messages based
// on a pressure reading read from a file.  Processing
// continues until the plant is evacuated because of
// a pressure reading over 100.

#include <iostream.h>
#include <fstream.h>

int main ()
{
    int  pressure;
    ifstream  data;
    data.open("Shell4.D1");

    /* LOOP TO BE FILLED IN */
        data  >> pressure;

        /* FILL IN Code to print the message */
    return 0;
}
```

Exercise 6: Examine program `Shell4`. When completed this program prompts for and reads an integer value and prints a warning message based on the input value.

Pressure	*Message*
< 0	"Error in input."
>= 0, < 50	"Pressure in the normal range."
>= 50, < 100	"Pressure on the high side."
> = 100	"Evacuate plant!!!!"

What kind of a loop is being used?

How many times was each message printed?

"Error in input."   _____

"Pressure in the normal range."   _____

"Pressure on the high side."   _____

"Evacuate plant!!!!"   _____

Exercise 7: The program to check pressure readings (your solution to Exercise 6) continues to run as long as the pressure readings are within the safe range. The program only halts when an unsafe reading is read. Plant maintenance has decided that the process should also be halted after 60 safe readings. Rewrite your solution from Exercise 6 to end the program when a dangerous reading occurs or when 60 safe readings have been read. Run your program twice, using `Shell4.D2` and `Shell4.D3` as input.

What was the result using `Shell4.D2`?

What was the result using `Shell4.D3`?

Exercise 8: Program `Shell4` as modified in Exercise 7 seems to be both an event-controlled loop and a count-controlled loop. However, we classify any loop that is not a pure count-controlled loop as an event-controlled loop. Explain why.

Exercise 9:   Plant maintenance has decided to add one more modification. If all the pressure readings are safe and there are less than 60 of them, stream **data** goes into the fail state. Rewrite the program so that it prints the message "Insufficient data." if there are less than 60 safe readings. Also print out how many pressure readings there were. Use the state of the input stream as the loop control. Run your program using **Shell4.D4**. How many pressure readings are there?

Lesson 2-3: Additional Control Structures

Exercise 1: As Pencil and Paper Self Check Exercise 4 demonstrated, program **Switches** is not very robust. Add code so that the program works properly with both lowercase and uppercase versions of the input letters. Run your program with the same data, but key the letters as lowercase.

Exercise 2: Program **Switches** is still not very robust. Add a default case that prints an error message and asks for the letter to be reentered. Test your program with the same data set, but add several letters that are not correct.

Exercise 3: Program **Shell5** is the shell of a program that counts all the punctuation marks in a file.

```
// Program Shell5 counts punctuation marks in a file.

#include <iostream.h>
#include <fstream.h>

int main ()
{
    ifstream  inData;
    char symbol;
    int   periodCt = 0;
    int   commaCt = 0;
    int   questionCt = 0;
    int   colonCt = 0;
    int   semicolonCt = 0;
    inData.open("switch.dat");
    /* FILL IN */
    return 0;
}
```

Fill in the missing code and run your program. Show the answers below.

Number of periods: _____   Number of commas: _____

Number of question marks: _____   Number of colons: _____

Number of semicolons: _____

Exercise 4: Add the code necessary for program **Shell5** to count blanks as well. How many blanks are there in file **switch.dat**? If you did not get 12, go back and check your program.

Use program **Looping** for Exercises 5 through 8. This program reads and sums exactly 10 integers and then reads and sums integers until a negative value is read.

```
// Program Looping uses a count-controlled loop to read and
// sum 10 integer values and an event-controlled loop to
// read and sum values until a negative value is found.
```

```
// The data is on file Looping.dat.
#include <iostream.h>
#include <fstream.h>
int main ()
{
    ifstream  inData;
    int   value;
    int   counter;
    int   sum;

    inData.open("Looping.dat");

    counter = 1;
    sum = 0;
    while (counter <= 10)
    {// ten values read and summed
        inData  >> value;
        sum = sum + value;
        counter++;
    }
    cout  << "The first sum is "  << sum  << endl;

    inData  >> value;
    sum = 0;
    while (value >= 0)
    {// values are read and summed until a negative is read
        sum = sum + value;
        inData  >> value;
    }
    cout  << "The second sum is "  << sum  << endl;
    return 0;
}
```

Exercise 5:   Compile and run program **Looping**.

First sum is _____.   Second sum is _____.

Exercise 6:   Program **Looping** contains two loops implemented with While statements. Rewrite program **Looping**, replacing the While statements with Do-While statements.

First sum is _____.   Second sum is _____.

Exercise 7:   Can program **Looping** be rewritten using a For statement for each loop? Explain.

Rewrite program **Looping** using a For statement to implement the count-controlled loop.

First sum is _____.   Second sum is _____.

Exercise 8: Rerun your program using data file `Looping.d2`. Describe what happens.

If an error condition was generated, correct your program and rerun the program.

First sum is _____. Second sum is _____.

Lesson 2-4   Test Plan

Exercise 1:   Design a test plan for program **HiScore** in Lesson 2-1, Exercise 6. (Hint: there should be at least six test cases.)

Reason for Test Case	*Input Values*	*Expected Output*	*Observed Output*

Exercise 2:   Implement the test plan designed in Exercise 1. You may show the results in the chart in Exercise 1.

Lesson 2-5   Debugging

Exercise 1:   Program `AddSub` is supposed to read in a letter and two integer values and print either the sum of the two values or the difference of the two values depending on the letter read. It is such a simple program, but it doesn't even compile! Correct the program and describe the errors.

Exercise 2:   Now that the program compiles, run it with the following sets of values.

Input Values	Means	What Is Printed
A 10 20	add 10 and 20	_____
A 20 10	add 20 and 10	_____
S 10 20	subtract 20 from 10	_____
S 20 10	subtract 10 from 20	_____

Exercise 3:   Unless you corrected the logic errors in Exercise 1, your answers are incorrect. Locate the logic errors and rerun your program until you get the correct answers. Describe the errors.

Exercise 4:   Program `Bugs` is supposed to sum the first ten values on a file and the second ten values on a file. The second ten values are a duplicate of the first ten, so the answers should be the same. The program checks to be sure that the file has been found and halts execution if the file is not found. Program `Bugs` compiles, says that the file cannot be found, but then the screen freezes. Can you find the problem? Describe it.

Exercise 5: Correct the problem and rerun the program. The file cannot be found, but now the program halts correctly. Correct the name of the file and rerun the program.

Exercise 6: What—the screen freezes again? Back to the drawing board. Describe the next error you find. Correct the program and run it again.

Exercise 7: Now you are getting output, but the answer is wrong for the second sum. When you find this last error, describe it, correct it, and rerun the program. What are the correct totals?

Programs from Scratch

Exercise 1: Your history instructor gives three tests worth 50 points each. You can drop one of the first two grades. The final grade is the sum of the best of the first two grades and the third grade. Given three test grades, write a program that calculates the final letter grade using the following cut-off points.

>= 90	A
< 90, >= 80	B
< 80, >= 70	C
< 70, >= 60	D
< 60	F

Exercise 2: Write a program to determine if the digits in a three-digit number are all odd, all even, or mixed odd and even. Your program should prompt the user to input a three-digit number and echo-print the number. If the digits in the number are all odd, write "This number contains all odd digits." If the digits are all even, write "This number contains all even digits." If the number contains both odd and even digits, write "This number contains both odd and even digits." Use integer division and modulus to access the digits in the number.

Exercise 3: The world outside of the United States has switched to Celsius. You are going to travel in the U.S., where the temperature is given in Fahrenheit. A friend said that a quick approximation of the Celsius equivalent of a Fahrenheit number is to take the number, subtract 32, and half it. Write a program that takes as input a temperature in Fahrenheit and calculates both the approximated Celsius equivalent and the actual Celsius equivalent. Write out all three values. If the approximation and the actual value are within two degrees, write out "Close enough." If they are not within two degrees, write out "Will not do."

Exercise 4: There is a temperature for which Fahrenheit and Celsius are the same. This value can be determined both algebraically and experimentally. Solve the problem algebraically first and then write a program that determines if a solution exists by experimentation.

Exercise 5: Write a program to print a triangle composed of a symbol. The number of lines in the triangle and the symbol should be entered as input from the keyboard. For example, if the input values are 7 and #, the output is as follows:

```
      #
     ###
    #####
   #######
  #########
 ###########
#############
```

In your program documentation, describe the loop(s) used as count-controlled or event-controlled.

Exercise 6: File `History.d1` contains a brief history of computing. There are no indentations in this file. Write a program to read this file, inserting five blanks at the beginning of each paragraph. You can recognize a paragraph because a blank line appears before the first line of each paragraph. Write the changed file on `History.d2`. In your program documentation, describe the loop(s) used as count-controlled or event-controlled.

Exercise 7: How many nonblank characters are there in file `History.d1`? Add a counter to your program from Exercise 6 that keeps track of the number of nonblank characters in the file. Print this number to the screen. Do not include '`\n`' in your nonblank count.

Exercise 8: As a child, did you ever play the game "One potato, two potato, . . ." to determine who would be "it?" The complete rhyme is given below:

One potato, two potato, three potato, four;
Five potato, six potato, seven potato, more.
O U T spells "out you go."

A child is pointed to during each phrase. There are four phrases in lines 1 and 2 and seven phrases in line 3, so the last child pointed to is the 15th one. If there are fewer than 15 children, you go around the circle again. The child pointed to when the word *go* is said is "out." The game begins again with the remaining children, starting again with the first child. The last child remaining is "it." Simulate this game in a computer program. The input is the number of children; the output is which child is "it."

Exercise 9: Modify the game in Exercise 8 so that rather than beginning again with child number 1, you start again with the child following the last one out.

Exercise 10: Write a program to analyze a sample of text. Collect statistics on the following categories of symbols:

- Uppercase letters
- Lowercase letters
- Digits
- End-of-sentence markers (periods, explanation points, and question marks)
- Intra-sentence markers (commas, semicolons, and colons)
- Blanks
- All other symbols

Use a Switch statement in your processing. (If you are not using the ASCII character set, you need to use functions found in `<ctype.h>`.)

After collecting these statistics, use them to approximate the following statistics:

- Average word length
- Average sentence length

Exercise 11: Design and implement a test plan for the program in Exercise 10.

Exercise 12: Scoring a tennis game is different from scoring any other game. The following table shows how a tennis game is scored. The first two points won by a player are worth 15 each, and the third point is worth 10. The score is always given with the server's score first. In this table, Player 1 is the server.

Score	Player 1 Wins Point	Player 2 Wins Point
0/0	15/0	0/15
0/15	15/15	0/30
0/30	15/30	0/40
0/40	15/40	game
15/0	30/0	15/15
15/15	30/15	15/30
15/30	30/30	15/40
15/40	30/40	game
30/0	40/0	30/15
30/15	40/15	30/30
30/30	40/30	30/40
30/40	30/30	game
40/0	game	40/15
40/15	game	40/30
40/30	game	30/30

The two underlined scores (30/30) should actually be 40/40, but in tennis you have to win by 2 points, so 40/40 behaves like 30/30. (See what we mean about being strange?) Write a function that takes two scores and the player who won the point and returns the new scores. This function is more complex than any you have done so far. Treat it like a complete program. Begin with a top-down design that outlines your solution. There are 15 possibilities, but some can be combined. You must use at least at least one Switch statement in your program.

Exercise 13: Write a test plan for the function written for Exercise 12. Implement your test plan.

CHAPTER

3

Functions, Scope, and Lifetime

OBJECTIVES

- To be able to write and invoke a parameterless void function to implement a specified task.
- To be able to write and invoke a void function with value parameters to execute a specified task.
- To be able to write and invoke a void function with reference parameters to execute a specified task.
- To be able to debug a program with a function.
- To be able to differentiate between static and automatic variables.
- To be able to define and invoke a numeric value-returning function to implement a specified task.
- To be able to define and invoke a Boolean value-returning function to implement a specified task.
- To be able to determine which variables are global, local, and nonlocal.

Functions

Identifiers can name actions as well as data objects. There are two types of named actions in C++: value-returning functions and void functions. The name of a value-returning function is used in an expression; the action is executed and the returned value is substituted in the expression. **sqrt** and **pow** are named actions that are value-returning functions. The name of a void function is used as a statement in the executable part of a program. The action is executed and the program continues with the statement immediately following the action name. The **get** in **cin.get** and the **open** in **inData.open** are void-function identifiers that name actions or processes. Both value-returning and void functions can be used to implement modules in a top-down design. In this chapter, we focus on how to write void functions.

Using the name of a function in an expression or as a statement is called *invoking* or *calling* the function.

Defining Void Functions

A void function has a heading that names the function and is followed by a pair of parentheses. (The function identifier is preceded by the word **void**.) A list of the identifiers that the function needs can be inserted within the parentheses. This list of identifiers is called a *parameter list*.

The parameter list on the function heading is called the *formal parameter list*. Each identifier on the formal parameter list must have its type listed. These identifiers are used in the statements in the executable part of the function. When the function is invoked, there is a list of identifiers in parentheses after the function name. This list of identifiers is called the *actual parameter list*. The identifiers on the actual parameter list name the places that the function actually uses during execution. The formal parameter list and the actual parameter list must match up in number and type because each actual parameter is substituted for its corresponding formal parameter when the function is executed.

Let's examine the syntax in the context of an example. Before we look at a function with parameters, let's look at the case where the function does not need any information from the outside and therefore has no parameter list. The task is to write a box that looks as follows:

```
. . , . . . . . . . . . . . . . . . . .
.                                     .
.                                     .
. . . . . . . . . . . . . . . . . . . .
```

There are 20 periods on the first line, 2 periods on the second and third lines separated by 18 blanks each, and the fourth line is identical to the first line. Function **WriteBox** produces this output.

```
void WriteBox()                 // name of the action
// Post: A box (20 x 4) is printed using periods.

{                                          // begin action
    cout << "...................." << endl;
    cout << "." << setw(19)  << "."  << endl;
```

```
        cout << "." << setw(19)  << "."  << endl;
        cout << "...................." << endl;
    }                                                // end action
```

The reserved word **void** precedes the name of the action. There is no parameter list, but the parentheses that enclose the parameter list must be present. The braces enclose the function body, the action part of the function. The four output statements write the box described above.

How does **WriteBox** get executed? The name of the action, **WriteBox**, is used as a statement in your program.

```
WriteBox();     // function invocation or 'call'
```

How does all this fit together? *Where* in the program? What *is* the program? A complete program containing function **WriteBox** is shown below. Notice that the function definition is set off with a row of asterisks before it. This design makes the parts of the program easier to distinguish for the human reader—the compiler doesn't care.

```
// Program Box writes a box using periods.

#include <iostream.h>
#include <iomanip.h>

void WriteBox();                          // function prototype
// Post: A (20 x 4) box of dots is written on the screen.

int main()
{
    cout << "A box: "  << endl;
    WriteBox();
    cout << "Box has been drawn."  << endl;
    return 0;
}

//************************************************

void WriteBox()                     // name of the action
// Post: A box (20 x 4) is printed using periods.

{                                                // begin action
  cout << "...................." << endl;
  cout << "." << setw(19)  << "."  << endl;
  cout << "." << setw(19)  << "."  << endl;
  cout << "...................." << endl;
}                                                // end action
```

Physical Order and Logical Order

The text of the function definitions can be in any physical order. The logical order of executing the compiled program begins with the first statement in function, **main,** which sends the characters "**A box:** " to the output stream. Function **WriteBox** is then executed. When function **WriteBox** is finished, control passes to the statement immediately following the call to **WriteBox**, and "**Box has been drawn.**" is sent to the output stream.

Most C++ programmers put function **main** first in the physical order of the program with the other function definitions following. Each function is separated by a row of some delimiter symbol. We use a row of asterisks. Because most C++ programs have function **main** listed first and each identifier must be declared before it is used, we have a problem. The functions invoked in function **main** are not known to the compiler because they have not been defined yet. We solve this dilemma by using a *function prototype* (also called a *function declaration*). A function prototype is the function heading without the body of the function. Look back at program **Box**; the comments identify the prototype for function **WriteBox**. Note that the function prototype ends with a semicolon, but the heading in the function definition does not.

Exiting a Function

We have seen with value-returning functions that the function is exited when a **return** statement is executed. That is, control is passed back to the place in the expression where the call occurred when a value is returned. How do you exit a void function? Control passes back to the statement immediately following the function call when the last statement in the function is executed or when a **return** that doesn't include an expression is executed. A **return** with no expression can occur only in a void function.

Functions with Parameters

Now, let's look at an example of a program with a function that has a parameter list.

```
// Program Demo prompts for and reads two integer
// values that represent the sides of a rectangle.
// The area of the rectangle is calculated and printed.

#include <iostream.h>

void GetData(int&, int&);                    // function prototype
// GetData gets two integer values.

int main()
{
    int   height;
    int   width;
    int   area;

    GetData(height, width);
    area = height * width;

    cout << "The area of the "  << height  << " by "
         << width  << " rectangle is "  << area  << endl;
    return 0;
}

//*****************************************************
```

```
void GetData(int& firstValue, int& secondValue)
// Post: The user has been prompted to input two values
//       representing the length and width of a rectangle.
//       These values have been read and returned in
//       firstValue and secondValue.
{
    cout  << "Enter two integer values representing "
          << "a rectangle.  Press return."  << endl;
    cin  >> firstValue  >> secondValue;
}
```

The identifiers on the formal parameter list of function **GetData** are **firstValue** and **secondValue**, which are both of type **int**. The identifiers on the actual parameter list are **height** and **width**. When function **GetData** is executed, **height** (the actual parameter) is substituted for **firstValue** (the formal parameter) and **width** (the actual parameter) is substituted for **secondValue** (the formal parameter). The names used on the formal and actual parameter lists are immaterial; the individual items are matched solely by position.

The function prototype can have the names of the formal parameters listed, but the compiler only needs to know the number of parameters and their data types. Therefore, the function prototype for **GetData** has just the data types listed. (We explain the ampersands in the next section.)

Value and Reference Parameters

In C++, there are two types of parameters: *value parameters* and *reference parameters*. If the formal parameter is a value parameter, a *copy* of the value of the actual parameter is passed to the function. If the formal parameter is a reference parameter, the *address* of the actual parameter is passed to the function. This means that if a value parameter is changed within a function, only the copy is changed. However, if a reference parameter is changed within a function, the actual parameter is changed. How can you tell which parameters are value and which are reference? Reference parameters have the ampersand (**&**) following their type identifier in the function prototype and function heading. Value parameters are the default parameter type, so they have nothing following their type identifiers.

The parameters for function **GetData** are reference parameters because the ampersand follows their type identifiers.

Parameters that send back values to the calling function are called output parameters (or outgoing). Parameters that only give information to the function are called input parameters (incoming). Parameters that both give information to the function and transmit information back are called in/out parameters (or incoming/outgoing). Output parameters and in/out parameters *must be reference parameters*. Input parameters should be value parameters so that the function cannot inadvertently change the actual parameter. C++ requires that all files must be passed as reference parameters.

The task of function **GetData** is to prompt for and read two integer values from the standard input stream. Because these values are needed by the calling function, they are reference parameters. If we change program **Demo** so that the last output statement is put into a function, **PrintData**, with three parameters (**height**, **width**, and **area**), should the parameters be value parameters or reference parameters? Because these values are not changed, they should be value parameters.

If a function needs no information and returns no values to the calling routine, then the function doesn't need parameters. Notice, however, that function prototypes, function headings, and function calls always must have the parentheses even if there are no parameters.

Local Variables

Any user-defined function is a heading and a body, and the body is a block. Therefore any function can include variable declarations. Declarations declared within a block are called *local variables*. Local variables are created when the function is called and disappear when the function finishes executing. Local variables are accessible only from within the block in which they are defined.

Documentation of Functions

There is a need-to-know principle in programming that says that the user of a function needs to know only *what* the function does, not *how* it does it. One way to implement this principle is to have the documentation on each function prototype state what the function does—just enough information for the program reader to understand the function's purpose. On the other hand, the documentation in the function heading and the body is for the person reading the details, usually the one responsible for maintaining the code. Therefore, the documentation in the function definition can state how the function is implemented.

As long as our programs are small enough to include all of the function definitions in the same file with function **main**, we use an informal style of documenting the function prototypes and definitions. In later chapters, when we separate the function prototypes and function definitions into different files, we use a more formal style in which preconditions describe the state of the parameters on input to the function and postconditions describe the state of the parameters on output from the function. Preconditions state what the function assumes is true on entry; postconditions state what the function guarantees to be true on exit from the function provided the preconditions are true. Preconditions and postconditions can be written in many different ways, ranging from simple English sentences to statements in formal logic.

In this formal documentation style, the function prototype becomes the *interface* to the function. It includes the formal description of the purpose of the function and a description of the parameters at the logical level. The implementation details are hidden within the definition of the function. The hiding of the implementation details within a separate block with a formally specified interface is called *encapsulation*. When our programs are large enough to warrant it, we use this style of documentation to emphasize encapsulation.

Data flow refers to information going into and out of a function. The direction of data flow can be documented by using one of the following statements as a comment beside each parameter in the prototype: 'in', 'out', 'in/out'. Note that 'out' and 'in/out' parameters must be designated as reference parameters.

✓ **Paper and Pencil Self Check #1**

Examine program **Stars** carefully.

```
// Program Stars prints NUM_STARS on the screen.

#include <iostream.h>

const int  NUM_STARS = 10;

void PrintStars();
// Prints NUM_STARS stars on the screen.

int main ()
{
    cout  << "The next line contains "  << NUM_STARS
          << " stars. "  << endl;
    PrintStars();
    PrintStars();
    return 0;
}
//****************************************************


void PrintStars ()
// Post: NUM_STARS asterisks are sent to cout.

{
    cout << "**********"  << endl;
    return;
}
```

Exercise 1: Show below exactly what program **Stars** writes on the screen.

Exercise 2: Trace the execution of program **Demo** in this chapter. The data is keyed as follows:

10 23

What is printed?

Exercise 3: If the values in the data line are entered in reverse order, what is printed?

Scope, Lifetime, and Value-Returning Functions

Local variables can be declared within *any* block—the block does not have to be the body of a function. In a large program, there may be several variables with the same identifier—*name*, for example. How do we know which variable is meant and where each variable is accessible? The answers to these questions are provided by scope rules.

Scope of an Identifier

There are three categories of scope for an identifier in C++: class scope, local scope, and global scope. Class scope is beyond the scope of this text. Local scope is the scope of an identifier defined within a block and extends from the point where the identifier is declared to the end of the block. Global scope is the scope of an identifier declared outside all functions and extends to the end of the file containing the program.

Function names in C++ have global scope. Once a function name has been declared, any subsequent function can call it. In C++ you cannot nest a function definition within another function. When a function defines a local identifier with the same name as a global identifier, the local identifier takes precedence. That is, the local identifier hides the existence of the global identifier. For obvious reasons this principle is called *name precedence* or *name hiding*.

The rules of C++ that govern who knows what, where, and when are called *scope rules*.

- A function name has global scope.
- The scope of a formal parameter is the same as the scope of a local variable declared in the outermost block of the function body.
- The scope of a local identifier includes all statements following the declaration of the identifier to the end of the block in which it is declared and includes any nested blocks unless a local identifier of the same name is declared in a nested block.
- The scope of an identifier begins with its most recent declaration.

The last two rules mean that if a local identifier in a block is the same as a global or nonlocal identifier to the block, the local identifier blocks access to the other identifier. That is, the block's reference is to its own local identifier.

To summarize, any variable or constant declared outside all functions is a *global identifier*. Any global identifier is known (and can be accessed directly) by any function that does not declare a variable or constant with the same name. Local identifiers of a function are *nonlocal* (but accessible) to any block nested within it.

If global identifiers are accessible to all functions, why don't we just make all identifiers global and do away with parameter lists? Good programming practice dictates that communication between the modules of our program should be explicitly stated. This practice limits the possibility of one module accidentally interfering with another. In other words, each function is given only what it needs to know. This is how we write "good" programs.

Lifetime of Variables

The *lifetime* of a variable is the time during program execution when the variable has storage assigned to it. The lifetime of a global variable is the entire execution of the program. The lifetime of a local variable is the execution of the block in which it is declared. There are times when we want to have the value of a local variable remain between calls to the same function. For example, if we want to know how many times a function is called during the execution of a program, we would like to use a local function variable as a counter and increment it each time the function is called. However, if space is allocated each time the function is called and deallocated when the function finishes executing, we can't guarantee that the space for the local variable is the same for each function invocation. In fact, it most likely would not be.

Therefore, C++ lets the user determine the lifetime of each local variable by assigning it a storage class: static or automatic. If you want the lifetime of a local variable to extend to the entire run of the program, you preface the data type identifier with the reserved word **static** when the variable is defined. The default storage class is automatic where storage is allocated on entry and deallocated on exit from a block.

Any variable may be initialized when it is defined. This is the fourth way to assign a value to a place in memory. To initialize a variable, follow the variable identifier with an equal sign and an expression. The expression is called an *initializer*. The initializing process differs depending on whether the variable being initialized is static or automatic. For a static variable, the initializer must be a constant expression, and its value is stored only once. For an automatic variable, the initializer can be any expression, and its value is stored each time the variable is assigned storage.

User-Defined Value-Returning Functions

With void functions, we use the function name with its parameters as a statement in our program to represent the action that the function performs. Value-returning functions are used when the action returns only one value and that value is used in an expression. For example, let's write a function that returns the smallest of its three input values.

```
// Program PrintMin prints the smallest of three input values.
#include <iostream.h>

int  Minimum(int, int, int);     // function prototype
// Returns the minimum of three distinct values.

int main()
{
    int one;
    int two;
    int three;
    cout  << "Input three integer values; press return."
          << endl;
    cin  >> one  >> two  >> three;
    cout  << "The minimum value of "  << one  << ", "
          << two  << ", and "  << three  << " is "
          << Minimum(one, two, three)  << "."  << endl;
    return 0;
}

//**********************************************************
```

```
int  Minimum(int first, int second, int third)
// Pre:  Input values are distinct.
// Post: Return minimum of three distinct int values.
{
    if (first < second && first < third)
        return first;
    else if (second < first && second < third)
        return second;
    else if (third < first && third < second)
        return third;
}
```

The function prototype declares a function of data type **int**. This means that the type of the value returned to the calling function is **int**. Because a value-returning function always sends back one value, we designate the type of the value before the function name. We usually call this data type the *function type*. Technically in C++, the function type is the function name, its argument list, and the return type. Therefore *function value type*, *function return type*, or *function result type* is more accurate for the type of the value returned from a value-returning function.

In this example, the function invocation occurs in the output statement in function **main**. Function **Minimum** is invoked and the value is returned and immediately sent to the output stream. There are three formal parameters: **first**, **second**, and **third**. The three actual parameters are **one**, **two**, and **three**. Notice that the documentation on the function prototype is different from the documentation on the function definition.

✓   **Paper and Pencil Self Check #2**

Read program **Scope** carefully and answer Exercises 1 through 6.

```
// Program Scope demonstrates scope rules and lifetime
// classes.

#include <iostream.h>
#include <fstream.h>

int   counter;
int   sum = 0;
int   number;

ifstream  inNums;

void  SumNumbers(ifstream&, int&);

int main ()
{
    inNums.open("Numeric.dat");
    {
        int  sum = 0;
        SumNumbers(inNums, sum);
        cout  << "Output from first call to SumNumbers"
              << endl;
        cout  << "Sum is "  << sum  << endl;
    }
```

```
        SumNumbers(inNums, sum);
        cout  << "Output from second call to SumNumbers"
              << endl;
        cout  << "Sum is "  << sum  << endl;
        return 0;
}
//************************************

void  SumNumbers(ifstream& inFile, int& answer)
{
        static int  counter = 1;
        while (counter <= 4)
        {
              inFile  >> number;
              answer = answer + number;
              counter++;
        }
}
```

Exercise 1:   File **Numeric.dat** contains the following values: 10 20 30 40 10 20 30 40. What is printed?

Exercise 2:   List the global identifiers.

Exercise 3:   Circle each of the blocks in program Scope and number them from top to bottom.

Exercise 4:   List the local identifiers and state the block(s) in which each is accessible.

Exercise 5:   List the automatic local variables.

Exercise 6:   List the static local variables.

Chapter 3: Assignment Cover Sheet

Name _____ **Date** _____

Fill in the following table showing which exercises have been assigned for each lesson and check what you are to submit: (1) lab sheets, (2) listings of output files, and/or (3) listings of programs. Your instructor or TA can use the Completed column for grading purposes.

Activities	Assigned: Check or list exercise numbers	Submit (1) (2) (3)			Completed
Laboratory Exercises					
Lesson 3-1: Functions					
Lesson 3-2: Scope, Lifetime, and Value-Returning Functions					
Lesson 3-4: Debugging					
Programs from Scratch					

Lesson 3-1: Functions

Use program Shell1 for Exercises 1 and 2.

```
// Program Shell1 is a program shell with a function.

#include <iostream.h>

void  Print();
// FILL IN the documentation.

main ()
{
    Print();
    return 0;
}

//*************************************

void  Print()
// FILL IN the documentation.
{
    /* TO BE FILLED IN */
}
```

Exercise 1:   Fill in the code for function **Print** so that it prints your name and address (on two separate lines) enclosed or boxed in dollar signs on the screen. Don't forget to fill in the appropriate documentation for function **Print**. Compile and run your program. Show your documentation.

Exercise 2:   Change function **Print** so that it reads the name and address from file **data.in**. Make your input file a reference parameter to function **Print**. Use '\n' to control your loops. You may assume that the name is on one line and the address is on the next line.   Compile and run your program. Show your documentation.   (Did you remember to change the documentation for function **Print**?)

Use program Shell2 for Exercises 3 through 5.

Writing boxes on the screen is fun. Program **Shell2** is the shell of a program that prompts the user to enter an integer number. When completed this number is read and passed to function **Print** as parameter **numSigns**. The function prints a box of dollar signs on the screen that is **numSigns** by (**numSigns** / 2). For example, if **numSigns** is 10, the following box is printed on the screen.

```
$$$$$$$$$$
$         $
$         $
$         $
$$$$$$$$$$
```

Note the interior dimensions are (**numSigns**-2) x (**numSigns** / 2-2).

```
// Program Shell2 prompts for the number of dollar signs for
// the top of the box.  That number / 2 - 2  lines are
// printed with dollar signs on the sides.

#include <iostream.h>

void  Print(int numSigns);
// FILL IN documentation.

int main ()
{
    int   number;

    cout  << "Enter the number of dollar signs for the top; "
          << "press return."
    cout  << "Enter end-of-file character to quit."  << endl;
    cin  >> number;
    while (cin)
    {
        /* FILL IN call to Print */
        cout  << "Enter the number of dollar signs for "
              << "the top; press return."
        cout  << "Enter end-of-file character to quit."
              << endl;
        cin >> number;
    }
    return 0;
}
//************************************
void  Print(int numSigns)
// FILL IN documentation.
{
    /* FILL IN code to print numSigns $'s */

    /* FILL IN code to print (numSigns / 2)-2 lines with   */
    /* $'s lining up under the left-most and right-most     */
    /* $ ones on the top line.                              */

    /* FILL IN code to print numSigns $'s                   */
}
```

Exercise 3: Fill in the missing code in function **Print** and the invoking statement in function **main** . Compile and run your program using 4, 10, and 7.

Exercise 4: Change your program so that when the number of dollar signs is odd, it uses (**numSigns** + 1) / 2 - 2

as the inside height dimension. Compile and run your program.

Exercise 5: Rewrite your solution to Exercise 4 so that the symbol used as the border is also read as data and passed to function **Print** as a parameter. To make the symbol a parameter requires the following changes:

- Prompt for and read the symbol.
- Add the symbol and its type (or just the type) to the formal parameter list of the function prototype.
- Add the symbol and its type to the formal parameter list of the function prototype.
- Add the symbol to the actual parameter list.

Run the program three times using &, %, and *A* as symbols and 4, 10, and 7 as the number of symbols to use.

Exercise 6: To complete this exercise look at program **Shell3**. This program reads two real numbers, **kilometers** and **hours**, and prints **kilometersPerHour** on the screen. Function **GetData** prompts the user for the appropriate values, reads them, and returns them to function **main**.

```
// Program Shell3 reads kilometers and hours and prints
kilometers
// per hour.
#include <iostream.h>
#include <iomanip.h>

/* FILL IN the function prototype for GetData */

int main ()
{
    float   kilometers;
    float   hours;
    float   kilometersPerHour;

    cout.setf(ios::fixed, ios::floatfield);
    cout.setf(ios::showpoint);
    /* FILL IN code to invoke function GetData */

    kilometersPerHour = kilometers / hours;
    cout  << setw(10)  << kilometers
          << setw(10)  << hours
          << setw(10)  << kilometersPerHour  << endl;
    return 0;
}
//*********************************************************

/* FILL IN the function heading for GetData */
{
    /* FILL IN Code to prompt for kilometers and hours */
    /* FILL IN Code to read kilometers and hours */
}
```

Fill in the missing code, and compile and run your program three times using the following values .

Kilometers	Hours	Kilometers per Hour
160.1	1.8	_____
332.0	4.5	_____
1250.0	100.5	_____

Exercise 7:   Run program **Shell3** three more times, entering the hours first and the kilometers second. Fill in the answers below.

Kilometers	Hours	Kilometers per Hour
1.8	160.1	_____
4.5	332.0	_____
100.5	1250.0	_____

Exercise 8:   Explain why the answers are different in Exercises 6 and 7.

Exercise 9:   Complete program **Shell4**. When completed, the program reads, counts, and averages the numbers stored in a file.

```
// Program Shell4 averages the values on file dataFile.

#include <iostream.h>
#include <fstream.h>

void ReadAndSum(ifstream&, int&, float&);
// Reads two integer values from a file.

int main ()
{
    ifstream  dataFile;
    int  numberOfValues;
    float  average;

    cout.setf(ios::fixed, ios::floatfield);
    cout.setf(ios::showpoint);
```

```
        dataFile.open("Shell4.dat");

        /* FILL IN the invoking statement for ReadAndSum */

        cout  << "The average of "  << numberOfValues
              << " values is "  << average  << endl;
        return 0;
}
//***************************************

void  ReadAndSum /* TO BE FILLED IN */
// FILL IN documentation.
{
    /* TO BE FILLED IN */
}
```

Fill in function **ReadAndSum** to read, count, and average all the numbers in **dataFile**. Run the program using the data on **Shell4.dat**.

List the Parameters   Reference or Value?

_____ _____

_____ _____

_____ _____

The average of _____ values is _____.

Exercise 10: Write a void function, **Count**, that takes a file name as input and returns the number of characters on the current line of the file. The function **main** should call the function within a loop that runs until the file stream fails (end of the file) and prints the answers on the screen. Test your program using **CharCt.d1**.

How many lines are there?

How many characters are there on each line?

Exercise 11: Write a void function, **FindMinimum**, that takes as input a file of integers and returns as output the minimum value on the file. (Remember that all file parameters must be passed by reference.) Write a **main** function that calls **FindMinimum** and prints out the minimum value. Use file **Numbers.dat**. What is printed?

Lesson 3-2: Scope, Lifetime, and Value-Returning Functions

Use program **Shell5** for Exercises 1 and 2.

```
// Program Shell5 is for investigating the differences between
// automatic and static variables.

#include <iostream.h>

void  TestLocals();

int main ()
{
    TestLocals ();
    TestLocals ();
    TestLocals ();
    return 0;
}

// ****************************************

void  TestLocals()
{
    /* TO BE FILLED IN */
}
```

Exercise 1: Function **TestLocals** defines an automatic variable, **count**, and initializes it to 1. The contents of **count** are incremented and sent to the output stream. Write this code and run program **Shell1**. Record your output. Was it what you expected?

Exercise 2: Change function **TestLocals** so that variable **count** is a static variable. Rerun your program and show your output. Was it what you expected?

Exercise 3: Explain the difference between the lifetime of an automatic variable and the lifetime of a static variable.

Exercise 4: Lesson 2-2, Exercise 4, contains a loop nested within a loop. The outer loop prompts for and inputs a digit. The inner loop sums the integers from zero through the digit. Rewrite your solution to this task so that the summing of the digits from zero through the input digit is done in an `int` function, `SumDigits`. The digit should be an input parameter. Rerun your changed version with the same data: 0, 3, 7, and 9. The results should be the same.

Exercise 5: Write an `int` function, `Minimum`, that finds the minimum value on a file. Write a `main` function that calls `Minimum` and prints out the minimum value. Use file `Numbers.dat`. What is printed?

Exercise 6: In Exercise 5, did you access the file name globally or did you pass the file name as a parameter to function `Minimum`? If you passed the file name, you had a reference parameter to a value-returning function. Both accessing a variable globally and having a reference parameter to a value-returning function are bad style. Should this function have been a void function with two reference parameters? Justify your answer.

Lesson 3-3: Debugging

Exercise 1: Program **Triangle** inputs three values representing the three sides of a triangle. If the three sides represent an equilateral triangle, "Equilateral" is printed. If the three sides represent an isosceles triangle, "Isosceles" is printed. If the three sides are all different, "Scalene" is printed. There is one problem: the program doesn't work. Debug it.

What errors did you find?

Show the last three lines of output.

Exercise 2: Look carefully at the last three answers. Did you notice that they are wrong? Yes, they have two equal sides—but they are not triangles at all! For the values to represent a triangle, the sum of any two must be greater than or equal to the third. Add this error checking to the program and print out a message stating that the sides do not represent a triangle. Show the last three lines of output.

Exercise 3: Program Triangle doesn't have any documentation or problem-specific identifiers. Add appropriate documentation and make the identifiers more meaningful. How did the lack of documentation and the poor choice of identifiers make debugging more difficult?

Exercise 4:   Function **Swap** takes two values as input and returns them in reverse order. This little utility routine is very useful. However, it doesn't seem to work correctly. Can you fix it? Program **Driver** is written to test function **Swap**. A program whose only purpose is to test a subprogram is called a *driver*. The driver reads in two values, calls **Swap** with the two input values, and writes out the result. Run **Driver** using 10 and 15 as the input values. What is printed?

Exercise 5:   This answer looks correct but the program has a bug in it—take our word for it. Search until you find an error, correct it, and run the program again. Describe the error. What is printed?

Exercise 6: We bet there is still a problem with your program. Keep on trying. What error did you find this time?

Programs from Scratch

Exercise 1:   The American Heart Association publishes brochures describing what it means to be "Heart Healthy." We should watch our cholesterol and make sure that no more than 30 percent of our calorie intake comes from fat. Write a program that reads all the food items eaten in a day along with the fat (in grams) and the calorie content. (Assume that each food item appears on a line by itself, with the fat and calories on the following line with a blank in between.) Echo-print your input on file `Diet.out`, followed by a statement that describes the day's food intake as heart healthy or not heart healthy.   Your program should be interactive. Be sure to modularize your program appropriately.

Exercise 2:   The following test plan is designed to test the program from Exercise 1. Execute this test plan. Because of the amount of input required to test this program, we have used a different format for the test plan.

```
General Cases
   Input¹
      food        : Egg McMuffin with orange juice and coffee.
      fat grams: 11
      calories : 360
      food        : Chunky chicken salad with iced tea.
      fat grams: 6
      calories : 198
      food        : Regular hamburger with small fries and diet
            coke.
      fat grams: 21
      calories : 476
   Expected Output
      input echo printed
      'Warning!  You had too many fat calories today.'
   Actual Output
```

```
   Input
      food        : Whole-grain cereal with low-fat milk and orange
                    juice.
      fat grams: 3
      calories : 280
      food        : Chunky chicken salad with iced tea.
```

---

[1]The nutritional information shown here came from a McDonald's placemat. Egg McMuffin, McLean Deluxe, and McDonald's are registered trademarks.

```
            fat grams: 6
            calories : 198
            food     : McLean deluxe, side salad, and diet coke.
            fat grams: 12
            calories : 375

        Expected Output
          input echo printed
          'Congratulations!  You had a Heart Healthy day.'
        Actual Output
```

```
End Cases
    Input
        food     : <eoln>
        fat grams: 0
        calories : 0
    Expected Output
        input echo printed with food taking up no characters
        'Congratulations!  You had a Heart Healthy day.'
    Actual Output
```

```
    Input
        food     : 47 A's
        fat grams: 0
        calories : 0
    Expected Output
        input echo printed with food taking up 46 characters
        'Congratulations!  You had a Heart Healthy day.'
    Actual Output
```

Exercise 3: You are going on a round-the-world trip and wonder how many miles you must cover to go from one time zone to another. Write a program that writes out a table showing how many statute miles you must cover to go from one time zone to another when you are at the equator, 30° N and S, 60° N and S, and 180° N and S. You may ignore any local time differences. You must use at least one void function.

Exercise 4: Alter the program you wrote in Exercise 3 so that it prints out both statute miles and nautical miles for the latitudes requested.

Exercise 5: Along with eating a heart healthy diet, everyone should get regular exercise. You are attending an aqua jogging class. After you have been jogging for 15 minutes, the instructor stops the class and has everyone take his or her pulse for six seconds. (She times you.) She then asks if you are in your target zone. To help the class out, you decide to program a target-zone calculator. Each person's target zone is between 60 percent and 75 percent of his or her predicted maximal heart rate in beats per minute. A good approximation to this maximal heart rate is 220 less the person's age.

Write a function, `InTheZone`, that takes a person's age and the six-second pulse rate and returns `true` if the person is within his or her zone and `false` otherwise. Keep prompting for and reading an age and a pulse rate until the user enters the end-of-file keystrokes. You must use at least one value-returning function in this assignment.

Exercise 6: Write a driver and a test plan for function `InTheZone`. Implement your test plan.

Exercise 7: In Chapter 2, Programs from Scratch Exercise 3, you were asked to create a table comparing Fahrenheit temperatures with the actual Celsius equivalent and an approximated equivalent. Redesign that program and use `float` functions to calculate the actual value and the approximated value. Run your program with the same data.

Exercise 8: Add a column to the table in Exercise 7 that shows the difference between the actual Fahrenheit equivalent and the approximation. This change makes use of value-returning functions as specified in Exercise 7 inappropriate. Rewrite the `float` functions as void functions and explain why value-returning functions are no longer appropriate.

Simple Data Types and Arrays

OBJECTIVES

- To be able to determine the range of numeric types.
- To be able to work with character data.
- To examine the results of using floating point arithmetic.
- To be able to define and use enumeration data types.
- To be able to distinguish between widening and narrowing in type coercion.
- To be able to define a one-dimensional array data type with integer indexes.
- To be able to declare a one-dimensional array variable with integer indexes.
- To be able to use a one-dimensional array variable with integer indexes.
- To be able to define a one-dimensional array data type with enumeration indexes.
- To be able to declare a one-dimensional array variable with enumeration indexes.
- To be able to use a one-dimensional array variable with enumeration indexes.
- To be able to pass arrays as parameters.
- To be able to apply subarray processing.
- To be able to use an array where the indexes have semantic content.
- To be able to define a two-dimensional array data type.
- To be able to read, store, and print values in a table (two-dimensional array variable).
- To be able to find the minimum value and the maximum value in a table.
- To be able to sum the individual rows of a table.

Simple Data Types

The built-in simple data types in C++ are integral types and floating types. The integral types are **char**, **short**, **int**, **long**, and **enum**. The floating types are **float**, **double**, and **long double**. You have seen all of these with the exception of the nonnumeric type **enum**, which we cover later in this chapter. All of these data types are called *simple* or *atomic* because they are composed of single, indivisible values.

The range of values that can be stored in a simple numeric data type depends on the number of bytes of storage assigned to the data type. C++ provides a unary operator, **sizeof**, that returns the number of bytes in its operand. C++ does not specify the number of bytes for any data type except **char**, which is defined to be one byte but guarantees that the following relationships are true.

```
1= sizeof(char)
<= sizeof(short)
<= sizeof(int)
<= sizeof(long)
```
and
```
   sizeof(float)
<= sizeof(double)
<= sizeof(long  double)
```

Numeric Constants

C++ allows three types of integral constants: decimal, octal, and hexadecimal. All of the integral constants we have used so far have been decimal. An octal constant begins with an explicit 0 (zero) and contains only the digits 0 through 7. A hexadecimal constant begins with an explicit 0 followed by either *x* or *X* and the digits in the number chosen from the set of digits 0 through 9 and the letters *A* through *F*, which represent the digits 0 through 15. For the rest of this manual, we use only decimal constants. Octal and hexadecimal constants are used in more advanced programming.

Floating point constants are assumed to be of data type **double**. If you want the constant to be of data type **float**, append an *f* or *F* to the end of the number.

Char Constants

Although data type **char** can be used to hold small integer values, its main purpose is to hold character data. Each character in a character set has two representations: an external and an internal. The external representation is what it looks like on an I/O device; the internal representation is the way in which it is encoded in memory. The external representation of the letter *B* is *B*; the internal representation is an integer value. The external representation of any character is the same in all character sets, but the internal representation is not. The internal representation of the letter *B* is 66 in ASCII and 194 in EBCDIC. When you send a variable to the output stream, how does it know whether to send the character or the number? If the variable is of data type **char**, the external representation is sent (printed). For any other integral type, a number is sent (printed).

There are two types of **char** constants: printable and nonprintable characters. The printable characters are listed in the text of a program enclosed in single quotes. The nonprintable characters, which are control characters used with hardware devices, are written in the program by their escape sequence. The escape sequence is one or more characters following a backslash (\). The most commonly used escape sequence is '\n' that forces a new line on an output device. In Chapter 2, an example of counting characters in lines of text used the expression (**character != '\n'**) to control a loop. That is, the loop executed as long as the character read was not the newline character '\n'.

Char Processing

Because data type **char** is considered a numeric data type, we can apply all the numeric operators to values of type **char**. Because we *can* does not mean we *should*. If you are using **char** variables to hold alphanumeric characters, adding two of them doesn't make sense. However, using them in relational expressions does make sense: we are making statements about the relationship between the two characters in terms of their relative positions in the collating sequence of the machine.

Compound conditions involving characters can be a problem depending on the character set of the machine. For example, if you want to test to see if a character is an uppercase letter, the following expression works correctly on an ASCII machine but not on an EBCDIC machine.

```
if (character >= 'A' && character <= 'Z')
```

In ASCII, the letters are sequential, but in EBCDIC there are several gaps between letters that are used to represent nonprintable characters. Therefore, **character** could contain a nonprintable character rather than an uppercase letter and the expression would still return true. To ensure that your programs are portable to any machine, you should use the collection of functions provided in **<ctype.h>** when working with character data. A few of the most useful functions are listed below:

isalpha(ch)	Returns true if **ch** is a letter; false otherwise.
isdigit(ch)	Returns true if **ch** is a digit; false otherwise.
iscntrl(ch)	Returns true if **ch** is a control character; false otherwise.
ispunct(ch)	Returns true if **ch** is a nonblank printable character (that is, not a letter or a digit); false otherwise.
toupper(ch)	Returns **ch** in uppercase regardless of original case.
tolower(ch)	Returns **ch** in lowercase regardless of original case.

Enumeration Types

An *enumeration type* is a type in which the constant identifiers (called *enumerators*) are explicitly listed.

```
enum Birds {BLUEJAY, CARDINAL, ROBIN, SEAGULL, SWALLOW};
enum LetterGrade {A, B, C, D, F};

Birds    aBird;
LetterGrade  grade;
```

`aBird` can contain any of the enumerators (constants) listed in data type `Birds`. `grade` can contain any of the enumerators listed in data type `LetterGrade`. The enumerators of an enumeration type can be used in a program just like any other constant.

```
aBird = ROBIN;
grade = A;
if (grade == B)
```

Note that `grade` does not contain the character *A*. `grade` contains a value of the data type `LetterGrade`, the enumerator *A*. For obvious reasons, enumeration types are called *user-defined* data types.

Enumerators are ordered by the way in which they are listed. In a relational expression enumerators are evaluated exactly as characters would be: whether one enumerator comes before the other in the ordering of the enumerators.

Stream I/O is not defined for enumeration types. Printing out the values of an enumeration type must be done by converting the value from the enumeration type into a string that corresponds to the enumerator.

```
switch (aBird)
{
    case BLUEJAY : cout << "BlueJay";
                   break;
    case CARDINAL: cout << "Cardinal";
                   break;
    .
    .
}
```

Values of an enumeration type cannot be read; they must be set in the program. However, the name of the enumeration type can be used to convert, or type cast, a number representing the position of an enumerator in the listing of the data type into the enumerator in that position. For example,

```
aBird = Birds(0)
```

stores **BLUEJAY** into variable **aBird** because **BLUEJAY** is in the 0th position of the enumerators. You can use this technique to input values of enumeration types. The user can be given a menu showing the enumerators and asked to key in the number representing the enumerator they wish to input. The number is read and type cast into the enumerator.

If you create an enumeration type that you might want to use again, you can store the definition in a file with the `.h` extension and use `#include` to access the file. Rather than putting the file name in angled brackets, you put it in double quotes. This tells the preprocessor to look for the file in your current directory.

More on Type Coercion and Type Conversion

Recall that *type coercion* is the implicit changing of a data type by C++ and *type conversion* is the explicit type changing by the programmer. Type coercion occurs whenever values of different data types are used in arithmetic and relational expressions, assignment operations, parameter passing, and as return values from value-returning functions.

In arithmetic and relational expressions, values of `char`, `short`, or `enum` data types are changed to values of type `int`. If all the data types involved are now type `int`, the expression is evaluated. If they are not all the same, the "lower" ones are promoted to the "highest" data type in the expression, and the expression is evaluated. The data types are ordered as follows from lowest (`int`) to highest (`long double`):

`int`, `unsigned int`, `long`, `unsigned long`, `float`, `double`, `long double`

Converting one data type to another that is higher is called *promotion* or *widening*. Notice that no information is lost.

When coercion occurs in assignment operations, parameter passing, and returning values from a value-returning function, a value is being stored into a variable. If the data type of the value and the variable are not the same, the value is coerced into the data type of the variable. If the data type of the variable is higher, then no information is lost, but it may be lost if the data type of the variable is lower. For example, if the function type is `int` and the value returned is `float`, the value is truncated. Converting a value from a higher to a lower data type is called *demotion* or *narrowing*.

Type coercion is defined from an `enum` type to an `int` type but not the other way around. You must use type conversion (type casting) to change an integer value into an enumerator. Look at the following statement.

```
aBird = Birds(aBird + 1);
```

`aBird` is coerced to `int` and 1 is added. However, the result must be type cast back to the enumeration type to be stored. Because this conversion is done at run time, there is no type checking. If `aBird` is equal to `SWALLOW` when this statement is executed, you do not get an error message.

Side Effects

C++ supplies a bewildering array of specialized operators that, like the control structures described in the last chapter, are nice to have but not necessary. We do not review them here, but we must take a few moments to review what we have called the basic *assignment operator*, a single equal sign, because all of the assignment operators behave in the same way.

A variable followed by an equal sign followed by an expression forms an *assignment expression*. Assignment expressions do two things: they calculate a value and (as a side effect) they store that value in the place named on the left of the equal sign. An assignment expression becomes an assignment statement when the expression is terminated by a semicolon. Because an assignment expression returns a value, it can be used within another expression. Thus,

```
if (value >= (one = one + 1))
```

calculates the value of `one + 1` and compares `value` to the result. As a side effect, variable `one` has the incremented value stored back in it. We mentioned in Chapter 2 that an assignment is actually an expression in the context of explaining what happens when the equal sign is used when the double equal is meant.

We are not advocating that you use assignment expressions embedded within other expressions in your program. Quite the contrary. We just want you to be aware that this type of statement is legal and what it means if you encounter it. Because this feature is so complex, hard to understand, and unnecessary, we do not recommend its use.

✓ ## Paper and Pencil Self Check #1

Exercise 1: Program `Gauge` reads `int` values and converts them to the appropriate constant in an enumeration type. The constants in the enumeration type are used as the case labels in a Switch statement that controls which message is printed.

```
// Program Gauge inputs pressure readings from file Gauge.dat
// and writes appropriate messages.

#include <iostream.h>
#include <fstream.h>

enum  DecisionType {ERROR, NORMAL, HIGH, EVACUATE};

void  GetPressure(ifstream&, DecisionType&);
// Gets variable of DecisionType from a file.

int main ()
{
    ifstream  readings;
    DecisionType  pressure;
    readings.open("gauge.dat");
    do
    {
        GetPressure(readings, pressure);
        switch (pressure)
        {
            case ERROR    : cout  << "Error in input."
                                  << endl;
                            break;
            case NORMAL   : cout  << "Pressure in normal range."
                                  << endl;
                            break;
            case HIGH     : cout  << "Pressure on the high side."
                                  << endl;
                            break;
            case EVACUATE : cout  << "Evacuate plant!!!!"
                                  << endl;
                            break;
        }
    } while (pressure != EVACUATE);
    return 0;
}

/****************************************************/

void GetPressure(ifstream& readings, DecisionType& pressure)
// Pre:  File readings has been opened.
```

```
// Post: An integer pressure has been read from file readings.
//       pressure is ERROR if a negative pressure was read.
//       pressure is NORMAL if the value was between 0 and 49.
//       pressure is HIGH if the value was between 50 and 99.
//       pressure is EVACUATE if the value was 100 or above.
{
    int  reading;

    readings  >> reading;
    if (reading < 0)
        pressure = ERROR;
    else if (reading < 50)
        pressure = NORMAL;
    else if (reading < 100)
        pressure = HIGH;
    else
        pressure = EVACUATE;
}
```

If file **Gauge.dat** has the following data values, what is printed?

10 1   49   50   99   -2   120

One-Dimensional Arrays

In addition to naming places and processes, an identifier can name a *collection of places*. When a collection of places is given a name, it is called a *structured data type* and is characterized by how the individual places within variables of the data type can be accessed.

A *one-dimensional array* is a structured data type in which a collection of places is given a name and the individual places are accessed by their position within the collection. There are two types associated with the array data type: the type of the items to be stored in the individual places in the structure and the type of the index used to specify the individual places within the structure. In C++, the type of the index must be an integral type.

```
const int MAX_ITEMS = 100;

int  numberList[MAX_ITEMS];
int  index;
```

numberList is an array variable that contains 100 **int** variables. An individual **int** variable within the array is accessed by giving the name of the array variable followed by its position (index). For example, **numberList[0]** accesses the first variable in the collection; **numberList[1]** accesses the second variable in the collection; and **numberList[MAX_ITEMS-1]** accesses the last variable in the collection. Notice that the items in the collection are indexed from zero through the number in the collection minus one. The following code segment would set all of the variables in the array variable **numberList** to zero.

```
for (index = 0; index < MAX_ITEMS; index++)
    numberList[index] = 0;
```

The index type can be any integral type. For example, we can define an array where the indexes are of an enumeration type **Birds** and the contents of the array are of type **int**.

```
const int MAX_BIRDS = 5;
enum  Birds {BLUEJAY, CARDINAL, ROBIN, SEAGULL, SWALLOW};

int  birdsSighted[MAX_BIRDS];
Birds  aBird;
int  index;
```

The following code segment sets all places in the array to zero.

```
for (aBird=BLUEJAY; aBird<MAX_BIRDS; aBird = Birds(aBird + 1))
    birdsSighted[aBird] =  0;
```

If the individual **int** values have all been set to zero, the following code segment reads and counts different types of birds until **cin** goes into the fail state (no more data).

```
cout  << "Enter a number between 0 and 4 representing a bird."
      << endl;
cin  >> index;
while (cin)
{
    aBird = Birds(index);
    birdsSighted[aBird] = birdsSighted[aBird] + 1;
    cout  << "Enter a number between 0 and 4"
          << " representing a bird."
          << endl;
    cin  >> index;
}
```

Notice that we read the value entered in the input stream as an **int** value and used the name of the enumeration type to convert it to an enumerator in that type. What would happen if the person at the keyboard accidentally keyed in the number 5? Unfortunately, the contents of what would be **birdsSighted[5]** (if it existed) probably would be accessed and incremented. The address of the first element in an array is called the *base address* of the array. To access a place in an array, the compiler generates the code to add the value of the index to the base address. If this calculation gives an out-of-bounds array index, the program does not notice and continues as if the reference were correct.

This type of error is hard to detect because it usually surfaces later in the program when a variable unrelated to an array reference has a wrong value. The moral here is to be very careful with array indexing expressions. The type of an index may be any integral type, but its value at run time must be between zero and the number of elements in the array minus one. If the index type is an enumeration type, the value must be a legitimate enumerator of the type.

There are no aggregate operations defined on arrays, but any operation that is defined on the component data type may be applied to items stored in an array.

Arrays as Parameters

Simple variables can be passed by value or by reference. Arrays are *always* passed by reference, so the ampersand indicating pass-by-reference is never used. The function to which the array is passed does not know its size, only its base address. Therefore, the number of elements in the array is usually passed as a parameter, and the code of the function ensures that only valid values are processed. Let's define a void function, **PrintBirds**, which takes array variable **birdsSighted** and prints out the number of each type sighted.

```
void PrintBirds(/* in */ int   birdsSighted[],
                /* in */ int   numOfTypes)
{
    int   i;

    for (i = 0; i < numOfTypes; i++)

        switch (Birds(i))
        {
            case BLUEJAY : cout << "Blue jays seen: "
                           << birdsSighted[BLUEJAY]  << endl;
                           break;
            case CARDINAL: cout << "Cardinals seen: "
                           << birdsSighted[CARDINAL]  << endl;
                           break;
            .
            .
            .

        }
}
```

The call to function **PrintBirds** would be

```
PrintBirds(birdsSighted, MAX_BIRDS);
```

The brackets on the formal parameter list alert the compiler that the actual parameter in that slot is to be the base address of an array variable. The processing within function **PrintBirds** uses the second parameter to determine how many items in the array are to be processed. It is up to the caller of the function to be sure that the actual parameters are consistent—that is, that the actual parameter for **numOfTypes** is the number of items in the actual parameter for **birdsSighted**.

For simple variables, we use value parameters when the actual parameter should not be changed. How can we protect incoming-only arrays from inadvertent changes if they are always reference parameters? If we insert the word **const** before the data type on the formal parameter list, the compiler does not let the function change the array parameter.

```
void PrintBirds(/* in */ const int birdsSighted[],
                /* in */ int numOfTypes)
```

Because the processing is controlled by the second parameter, it can be the size of the array if all the elements are used or the number of data values that are actually stored if fewer values are stored than the size calls for. The latter type of processing is called *subarray* processing.

Initialization of Arrays

Just as we can initialize values within the definition of a simple variable, we can initialize array variables. The following declarations initialize each item in the array **birdsSighted** to zero.

```
const int MAX_BIRDS = 5;
enum  Birds {BLUEJAY, CARDINAL, ROBIN, SEAGULL, SWALLOW};

int  birdsSighted[MAX_BIRDS] = {0, 0, 0, 0, 0};
```

If this declaration is within a function other than **main**, **birdsSighted** is initialized each time the function is called. If **birdsSighted** is declared within a function and has the reserved word **static** before the **int**, it is initialized only once.

✓ ## Paper and Pencil Self Check #2

Exercise 1: Read program **Arrays** carefully.

```
// Program Arrays manipulates values in an array.
#include <iostream.h>

int main ()
{
    const int MAX_ARRAY = 5;
    int  numbers[MAX_ARRAY];
    int  index;
    int  sum;

    // Store values in the array.
    for (index = 0; index < MAX_ARRAY; index++)
        numbers[index] = index * index;

    // Sum values in the array.
    sum = 0;
```

```
      for (index = 0; index < MAX_ARRAY; index++)
          sum = sum + numbers[index];
      cout  << "Sum is "  << sum  << endl;
      return 0;
  }
```

Describe what is written on the screen.

Exercise 2: What would happen if the For loop headings were changed as follows?

```
for (index = 0; index <= MAX_ARRAY; index++)
```

Two-Dimensional Arrays

A *two-dimensional array* is a collection of components of the same type that is structured in two dimensions. Individual components are accessed by their position within each dimension. Three types are associated with a two-dimensional array data type: the type of the items to be stored in the individual places in the structure, the type of the index for the first dimension, and the type of the index for the second dimension. In C++ the type of both dimensions must be integral.

```
const int MAX_ROWS = 10;
const int MAX_COLUMNS = 5;

typedef float ItemType;

ItemType  twoDimAry[MAX_ROWS][MAX_COLUMNS];
```

twoDimAry is an array variable that has 10 rows and 5 columns. Each row and column entry is of type **float**. The following code fragment sets all the entries in **twoDimAry** to zero.

```
for (int column = 0; column < MAX_COLUMNS; column++)
    for(int row = 0; row < MAX_ROWS; row++)
        twoDimAry[row][column] = 0.0;
```

Table Processing

Just as a one-dimensional array data type is the structure used to represent items in a list, a two-dimensional array data type is the structure that is often used to represent items in a *table*. The number of rows and columns in the two-dimensional array variable is fixed at compile time. The number of rows and columns in the table can vary as the program executes. Therefore, each dimension should have a length parameter associated with it that contains the number of rows or columns actually used.

Processing a table requires two loops: one for the rows and one for the columns. If the outer loop is the index for the column, the table is processed by column. If the outer loop is the index for the row, the table is processed by row. The loop above processes **twoDimAry** by columns.

Multidimensional Arrays

You have seen one-dimensional and two-dimensional arrays. In C++, arrays may have any number of dimensions. To process every item in a one-dimensional array, you need one loop. To process every item in a two-dimensional array, you need two loops. The pattern continues to any number of dimensions. To process every item in an *n*-dimensional array, you need *n* loops.

Passing Arrays as Parameters

We said that the programmer passes the base address of an array and the number of elements in the array as parameters. The function does not need to know the actual size of the array. For arrays of more than one dimension, the function must know the sizes of all of the dimensions except the first. For example, if a function is defined to set the first **num** values of each row in **twoDimAry** to a specific value, the prototype might look like this:

```
void SetSomeVals(/* out */ ItemType twoDimAry[][MAX_COLUMNS],
                 /* in */  int rowsUsed,
                 /* in */  int num,
                 /* in */  ItemType initialValue);
```

Any actual parameter must have exactly the same number of elements specified for the second dimension. If it does not, the program continues but does not initialize the correct locations. It is safer to define a type using a Typedef statement, put the type name on the formal parameter list, and define the actual array to be of that type. Here is an example.

```
const int MAX_ROWS = 10;
const int MAX_COLUMNS = 5;
typedef char ItemType;

typedef ItemType TableType[MAX_ROWS][MAX_COLUMNS];

void SetSomeVals(/* out */ TableType twoDimAry,
                 /* in */  int rowsUsed,
                 /* in */  int num,
                 /* in */  ItemType initialValue);
```

Any array to be passed to **SetSomeVals** should be defined to be of type **TableType**. Although this example is of a two-dimensional array, this pattern of defining a type and using the type name can be used for arrays of any number of dimensions.

✓ **Paper and Pencil Self Check #3**

Exercise 1:   What does the following code segment print if **MAX_ROWS** is 10 and **MAX_COLS** is 10? Fill in the table shown below the code.

```
rowsUsed = 5;
colsUsed = 5;

for (int column = 0; column < MAX_COLS; column++)
    for (int row = 0; row < MAX_ROWS; row++)
        table[row][column] = '*';

for (row = rowsUsed; row < MAX_ROWS; row++)
    for (column = colsUsed; column < MAX_COLS; column++)
        table[row][column] = '+';

for (column = 0; column < colsUsed; column++)
    for (row = 0; row < rowsUsed; row++)
        table[row][column] = '-';
```

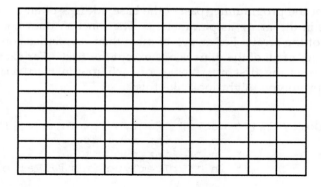

Exercise 2:   Is the first nested For loop in Exercise 1 processing the table by row or by column?

Is the second nested For loop processing the table by row or by column?

Is the third nested For loop processing the table

Chapter 4: Assignment Cover Sheet

Name_____ Date_____

Fill in the following table showing which exercises have been assigned for each lesson and check what you are to submit: (1) lab sheets, (2) listings of output files, and/or (3) listings of programs. Your instructor or TA can use the Completed column for grading purposes.

Activities	Assigned: Check or list exercise numbers	Submit (1)	(2)	(3)	Completed
Laboratory Exercises					
Lesson 4-1: Simple Data Types					
Lesson 4-2: One-Dimensional Arrays					
Lesson 4-3: Two-Dimensional Arrays					
Lesson 4-4: Debugging					
Programs from Scratch					

Lesson 4-1: Simple Data Types

Exercise 1:   Write a program that prints out the followings values:

        INT_MAX
        1 + INT_MAX
        1 + (- INT_MAX)
        1 - INT_MAX
        1 - (- INT_MAX))

In order to access **INT_MAX**, you must include file **<limits.h>**. Did you get what you expected? Explain.

Exercise 2:   Examine the following program.

```
// Program FactTest is a driver program that tests function
// Factorial.

#include <iostream.h>

int  Factorial(int);
// Calculates factorial of an integer.

int main ()

{
    int   number;

    cout  << "Enter a nonnegative integer number. "
          << "Press return."  << endl;
    cin  >> number;
    while (number >= 0)
    {
        cout  << number  << " factorial is "
              << Factorial(number)  << endl;
        cout  << "To continue, enter another nonnegative "
              << "number; to quit, enter a negative number."
              << endl;
        cin  >> number;
    }
    return 0;
}

/*************************************************************/

int  Factorial(int  number)
// Pre:  number is positive.
// Post: Return value is the factorial of number, calculated
//       iteratively.
```

```
{
    int  tempFact = 1;

    while (number > 1)
    {
        tempFact = tempFact * number;
        number = number - 1;
    }
    return tempFact;
}
```

The factorial of 0 is 1; the factorial of a positive integer is the product of the numbers from 1 up to and including the integer. For example, the factorial of 4 is 4*3*2*1, or 24. Program **FactTest** is a driver for function **Factorial**, which computes the factorial of an input value. Compile and run this program using increasing integer values beginning with zero. Record the input values along with the associated factorials until something strange happens.

Value	*Factorial*	*Value*	*Factorial*
_____	_____	_____	_____
_____	_____	_____	_____
_____	_____	_____	_____
_____	_____	_____	_____
_____	_____	_____	_____

Factorials build up very quickly. When the value being calculated gets too large to be stored in a memory location in your particular computer (greater than **INT_MAX**), overflow occurs. Each system handles it differently. Describe what happens on your system. Relate the results to the answers to Exercise 1.

Exercise 3: Change function **Factorial** to be of type **long** and rerun your program. What is the largest factorial that can be computed using type **long**?

Exercise 4: **Shell1** is the shell of a program designed to read characters and process them in the following way.

lowercase character	converts to uppercase and writes the character
uppercase character	writes the character
digit	writes the digit
blank	writes a blank
newline	writes newline
any other character	does nothing

```
// Program Shell1 reads characters from file DataIn and
//      writes them to DataOut with the following changes:
//      all letters are converted to uppercase, digits are
//      unchanged, and all other characters except blanks and
//      newline markers are removed.

#include <iostream.h>
#include <ctype.h>
#include <fstream.h>

int main ()
{
    ifstream  dataIn;
    ofstream  dataOut;
    char  character;

    dataIn.open("ReFormat.dat");
    dataOut.open("DataOut.dat");

    dataIn.get(character);     // priming read
    while (dataIn)
    {
        /* FILL IN THE Code to output the correct character */
        dataIn.get(character);
    }
    return 0;
}
```

You are to fill in the code to make the required conversions and create the output file. Run your program. List below the last three lines of output written on file **DataOut**.

Exercise 5: **Shell2** is the shell of a program that solves the problem in Exercise 4, using an enumeration data type.

```
// Program Shell2 reads characters from file DataIn and
// writes them to DataOut with the following changes:
//      all letters are converted to uppercase, digits are
//      unchanged, and all other characters except blanks and
//      newline markers are removed.
#include <iostream.h>
#include <ctype.h>
#include <fstream.h>
```

```
enum CharType {LO_CASE, UP_CASE, DIGIT, BLANK_NEWLINE, OTHER};

CharType  KindOfChar(char);
// Gets the enumerator equivalent to its character input.
int main ()
{
    ifstream  dataIn;
    ofstream  dataOut;
    char  character;

    dataIn.open("ReFormat.dat");
    dataOut.open("DataOut.dat");

    dataIn.get(character);     // priming read
    while (dataIn)
    {
        switch (KindOfChar(character))
        {

            // FILL IN THE Code to output the correct character

        }
        dataIn.get(character);
    }
    return 0;
}


/****************************************************/

CharType  KindOfChar(char  character)
// Post: character has been converted to the corresponding
//       constant in the enumeration type CharType.
{
    if (isupper(character))
        return  // TO BE FILLED IN
    else if (islower(character))
        return  // TO BE FILLED IN
    else if (isdigit(character))
        return  // TO BE FILLED IN
    else if (character == ' ' || character == '\n')
        return  // TO BE FILLED IN
    else
        return  // TO BE FILLED IN
}
```

You are to fill in the code of function **KindOfChar** and the Switch statement in
the body of function **main**. Run your program. List below the last three lines of
output written on file **DataOut**.

Lesson 4-2: One-Dimensional Arrays

Use program Reverse for Exercises 1 through 3.

```
// Program Reverse reads numbers into an array
// and prints them out in reverse order.

#include <iostream.h>
#include <fstream.h>

const int MAX = 10;

int main ()
{
    int   numbers[MAX];
    ifstream  inData;
    int   value;
    int   index;

    inData.open("reverse.dat");
    for (index = 0; index < MAX; index++)
    {
        // FILL IN Code to read value
        // FILL IN Code to store value into numbers
    }

    for (index = MAX - 1; index >= 0; index--)
        // FILL IN Code to write numbers on the screen
    return 0;
}
```

Exercise 1: Complete the missing code in program **Reverse** and run it. What is printed on the screen?

Exercise 2: Exercise 1 asked you to fill in the body of the first For loop with two statements. Replace these two statements with a single statement and rerun your program; your answer should be the same. If it is not, correct your code and rerun the program. Describe any problems that you had.

Exercise 3: Extend the program in Exercise 2 to print the sum of the values stored in **numbers**. What is the sum?

Use program Favorit for Exercises 4 through 6.

```
// Program Favorit determines the favorite soft drink.

#include <iostream.h>

enum  DrinksType {COKE, PEPSI, SPRITE, DR_PEPPER};
void Prompt();

int main ()
{
    int   sums[4];
    int   number;
    DrinksType   index;

    for (index = COKE; index <= DR_PEPPER; index =  DrinksType(index+1))
       // FILL IN Code to set sums to zero

    Prompt();
    cin  >> number;
    while (number != 4)
    {
         // FILL IN Code to increment the proper drink
       Prompt();
       cin  >> number;
    }

    // FILL IN THE Code to write out the totals
    return 0;
}

/************************************************************/

void Prompt()
{
    cout  << "Enter a 0 if your favorite drink is a Coke."
          << endl;
    cout  << "Enter a 1 if your favorite drink is a Pepsi."
          << endl;
    cout  << "Enter a 2 if your favorite drink is a Sprite."
          << endl;
    cout  << "Enter a 3 if your favorite drink is a DrPepper."
          << endl;
    cout  <<"Enter a 4 if you wish to quit the survey."
          << endl;
}
```

Exercise 4: Complete program **Favorit** and run it. What data did you use? What did the program write?

Exercise 5:   Add a function to program **Favorit** that sums the number of responses to the survey. Pass the array **sums** as a parameter. Print the number of responses on the screen. Run the program with the same data you used in Exercise 1. How many responses were there?

Exercise 6:   Add a function that takes the array **sums** as a parameter and prints the percentage of responses each drink received. Run your program on the same data. Show the results.

Lesson 4-3: Two-Dimensional Arrays

This lesson uses program **TwoDim**.

```
// Program TwoDim manipulates a two-dimensional array
// variable.
#include <iostream.h>
#include <fstream.h>

const int ROW_MAX = 8;
const int COL_MAX = 10;
typedef int ItemType;
typedef ItemType TableType[ROW_MAX][COL_MAX];

void  GetTable(ifstream&, TableType, int&, int&);
// Reads values and stores them in the table.
void  PrintTable(ofstream&, const TableType, int, int);
// Writes values in the table to a file.

int  main ()
{
    TableType  table;
    int  rowsUsed;
    int  colsUsed;
    ifstream  dataIn;
    ofstream  dataOut;

    dataIn.open("twod.dat");
    dataOut.open("twod.out");
    GetTable(dataIn, table, rowsUsed, colsUsed);
    PrintTable(dataOut, table, rowsUsed, colsUsed);
    return 0;
}

//****************************************************

void  GetTable(ifstream&  data, TableType  table,
               int&  rowsUsed, int&  colsUsed)
// Pre:  rowsUsed and colsUsed are on the first line of
//       file data; values are one row per line
//       beginning with the second line.
// Post: Values have been read and stored in the table.
{
    ItemType  item;
    data  >> rowsUsed >> colsUsed;

    for (int row = 0; row < rowsUsed; row++)
        for (int col = 0; col < colsUsed; col++)

            // FILL IN Code to read and store the next value.
}

//****************************************************

void  PrintTable(ofstream&  data, const TableType  table,
                 int  rowsUsed, int  colsUsed)
// Pre:  The table contains valid data.
// Post: Values in the table have been sent to a file by row,
```

```
//        one row per line.
{

    // FILL IN Code to print table by row.

}
```

Exercise 1: Read the documentation carefully and complete program `TwoDim`. Show what is printed.

____ ____ ____ ____ ____

____ ____ ____ ____ ____

____ ____ ____ ____ ____

____ ____ ____ ____ ____

Exercise 2: Add a function that prints the largest value in `table`. Rerun the program.

Largest value _____

Exercise 3: Add a function that prints the smallest value in `table`. Rerun the program.

Smallest value _____

Exercise 4: Add a function that sums the values in a column of `table`. Pass the column you want to sum as a parameter. Call your function to print the sum of each column appropriately labeled.

Sum of Col. 1 _____ Sum of Col. 2 _____   Sum of Col. 3 _____

Sum of Col. 4 _____ Sum of Col. 5 _____

Exercise 5: The specifications on the data have been changed. The data is to be entered one column per line instead of one row per line. In addition, the order of `rowsUsed` and `colsUsed` has been reversed; that is, `colsUsed` is the first value on the first line and `rowsUsed` is the second value. Rewrite function `GetTable` to input `table` using the new specifications. Run your program using `twodalt.dat`.

Smallest value _____   Largest value _____

Sum of Col. 1 _____ Sum of Col. 2 _____   Sum of Col. 3 _____

Sum of Col. 4 _____ Sum of Col. 5 _____

Lesson 4-4: Debugging

Exercise 1: Program **ReadData** reads data into a two-dimensional array. The data is input as described in program **TwoDim** in Lesson 4-3. The data file is shown below:

```
3   4
1   2   3   4
5   6   7   8
9   8   7   6
```

Unfortunately, program **ReadData** contains an error. Can you find and fix it? Describe the error.

Exercise 2: Unless you found two errors at once in Exercise 1, there is still an error lurking in program **ReadData**. Correct the error and rerun the program. Describe the error.

Programs from Scratch

Exercise 1: Design and implement a program to analyze a sample of text. Collect statistics on the following categories of symbols:

- Uppercase letters
- Lowercase letters
- Digits
- End-of-sentence markers (periods, explanation points, and question marks)
- Intrasentence markers (commas, semicolons, and colons)
- Blanks
- All other symbols

Use a Switch statement in your processing where the cases are constants in an enumeration type. (If you are not using the ASCII character set, you need to use functions found in `<ctype.h>`.)

After collecting these statistics, use them to approximate the following statistics:

- Average word length
- Average sentence length

Exercise 2: Design and implement a test plan for the program in Exercise 1.

Exercise 3: Chapter 2, Programs from Scratch Exercise 12, asked you to score a tennis match. Recall that scoring a tennis game is different from scoring any other game. The following table shows how a tennis game is scored. The score is always given with the server's score first. In this table, Player 1 is the server.

Score	Player 1 Wins Point	Player 2 Wins Point
0/0	15/0	0/15
0/15	15/15	0/30
0/30	15/30	0/40
0/40	15/40	game
15/0	30/0	15/15
15/15	30/15	15/30
15/30	30/30	15/40
15/40	30/40	game
30/0	40/0	30/15
30/15	40/15	30/30
30/30	40/30	30/40
30/40	<u>30/30</u>	game
40/0	game	40/15
40/15	game	40/30
40/30	game	<u>30/30</u>

The two underlined scores (30/30) should actually be 40/40, but in tennis you have to win by 2 points, so 40/40 behaves like 30/30. (See what we mean about being strange?)

You were asked to write a function that takes two scores and the player who won the point and returns the new scores. Rewrite your solution making the players an enumeration type.

Exercise 4: Write a program to grade a set of true/false tests. There are 15 true/false questions. True is represented by *T*, and false is represented by *F*. The key to the quiz is on file **Quiz.dat** followed by the student responses. Each student's name (maximum of 15 characters) immediately follows the student's last answer. For each student write out the name followed by the number answered correctly and the number missed. Use stream failure to terminate processing.

Exercise 5: An organization that your little cousin belongs to is selling low-fat cookies. If your cousin's class sells more cookies than any other class, the teacher has promised to take the whole class on a picnic. Of course, your cousin volunteered you to keep track of all the sales and determine the winner.

Each class has an identification number. Each sales slip has the class identification number and the number of boxes sold. You decide to create two arrays: one to hold the identification numbers and one to record the number of boxes sold. The identification numbers range from 1 through 10. Here is a sample of the data.

Id. Number	Boxes Sold
3	23
4	1
2	13
2	7
4	5
1	6
10	16
.	
.	

The first time an identification number is read, store it in the next free slot in the array of identification numbers and initialize the corresponding position in the array of boxes sold to the number sold on the sales slip. Each subsequent time an identification number is read, add the number of boxes sold to the corresponding position in the array of boxes sold.

When there are no more sales slips, scan the array of boxes sold for the largest value. The identification number in the corresponding position in the array of identification numbers is the class that wins.

Write your program and run it using data file **Boxes.dat**. Which class won and how many boxes of cookies did they sell?

Exercise 6: In Exercise 5, the class identification numbers range from 1 through 10. If they ranged from 0 through 9, the identification number could be used as an index into the array of boxes sold. Using this scheme, you need only one array to hold the boxes sold. Rewrite your program implementing this scheme. You can use the same data file by always subtracting one from the identification number on input and adding one to the identification number on output. Run your program using **Boxes.dat**. You should get the same results as in Exercise 5. Did you?

Exercise 7: Write test plans for Exercises 5 and 6. Can these test plans be the same, or must they be different? Explain.

Exercise 8: If an index has meaning beyond simply indicating the place in the collection, we say that it has *semantic content*. Exercise 6 is an example of processing in which the array indexes have semantic content. Explain.

Exercise 9: Two-dimensional arrays are good structures to represent boards in games. Write a function that takes a two-dimensional array as input and marks the array as a checkerboard. Put an asterisk in the black squares and a blank in the white squares. Write a second function that prints the checkerboard on the screen. Because a checkerboard is a fixed size, the dimensions of the board may be set as constants and accessed nonlocally.

Exercise 10: Write a program that keeps track of stock prices for five stocks for one week. Choose any five stocks on the New York Stock Exchange. Use actual stock prices for one week as your data. Include the clippings from the paper with your program.

Your program should be interactive. Prompt the user to enter the names of the five stocks. Then prompt the user to enter a week's worth of prices for each stock. The program should print the table showing the stock values for a week, the average daily value of the stocks, and the average price for each stock for the week.

Exercise 11: A two-dimensional array is the ideal structure to represent a matrix. Write the following functions, which implement the matrix operations add and subtract. In order to test your operations, you need a function to read values from a file and store them in a matrix and a function to write the values in a matrix on a file. Let your matrices be 5 by 4.

Add	Takes two matrices (**A** and **B**) as input and returns a matrix (**Result**) in which each position is the sum of the corresponding positions in **A** and **B**.
Sub	Takes two matrices (**A** and **B**) as input and returns a matrix (**Result**) in which each position is the corresponding position in **A** minus the corresponding position in **B**.
Write	Takes a file name and a matrix as input and writes the matrix by row, one row per line on the file.
GetMat	Takes a file name and a matrix as input and reads values from the file and stores them into the matrix.

Exercise 12: Write and implement a test plan for the matrix operations you wrote in Exercise 11.

Paper and Pencil Self Check Answers[1]

Chapter 1

SELF CHECK #1

Exercise 1:   You spend 7 hours and 15 minutes a day on scheduled activities.

Was your answer completely correct? If it was not, can you explain where you made your mistake?

Exercise 2:   The identifiers are `totalMinutes`, `DRESS`, `EAT`, `DRIVE`, and `CLASS`.

Exercise 3:   The named constants are `DRESS`, `EAT`, `DRIVE`, and `CLASS`.

Exercise 4: 0, 2, 3, 4, 30, 45, 60 are the numeric literal constants. `"You spend "`, `" hours and "`, and `" minutes a day on scheduled activities."` are string literals.

Exercise 5: `cout` and `endl` are defined in `<iostream.h>`.

SELF CHECK #2

Exercise 1:   19 35 4 6

Were your answers completely correct? If they were not, can you explain what was wrong.

Exercise 2:
```
1066
1069
      1069          1069106
1069.141479
  1069.141
1069.141
10691069    1069
```

Were your answers completely correct? If they were not, can you explain what was wrong.

Exercise 3:
 intValue = INT NUMBER + FLT NUMBER;

    fltValue = float(INT_NUMBER) + FLT_NUMBER;

---

[1]The programs used in the Paper and Pencil Self Check Sections are on the disk.

SELF CHECK #3

Exercises 1:

```
8.799999
7.7
6.6
5.5
```

Did one of the answers surprise you? Can you explain it?

Exercises 2 and 3: Program **Frame** expects two lines of input. You can tell because there are two accesses to **cin** with an output statement in between.

What happened when you keyed both numbers on the same line? The prompt for the horizontal dimension was given even though the value had been input. The answer was correct.

top side		centimetersOfWood
10	20	60
13	5	36
12	12	48

Were your hand simulations correct? If not, do you know why not?

Exercise 4: The program works correctly in both cases. Programs **Frame2** and **Frame3** input the data as described in parts a and b of this exercise, respectively. Were your answers completely correct? If not, explain where you made your mistake(s).

Exercise 5: The program would input the combined numbers as one and store it in the first place named on the input statement (**side**). The program would then wait for the next value to be input.

Exercise 6: Compare your answers with program **Frame4**, which has the changes requested.

```
// Program Frame4 reads input values that represent the
// dimensions of a print from a file and calculates and
// prints the amount of wood needed for a frame.

#include <iostream.h>
#include <fstream.h>


int main ()
{
    ifstream  din;      // input stream
    int  side;          // vertical dimension in centimeters
    int  top;           // horizontal dimension in centimeters
    int  centimetersOfWood; // centimeters of wood needed

    din.open("Frame.In");
    din  >> side  >> top;
    cout  << "Dimensions are " << top  << " and "
         << side  << "."  << endl;
```

```
            centimetersOfWood = top + top + side + side;

            cout  << "You need "  << centimetersOfWood
                  <<" centimeters of wood."  << endl;
            return 0;
}
```

Chapter 2

SELF CHECK #1

Exercise 1:
```
Temperature to convers: 100
Converted temperature: 212
```

Was your answer completely correct? If it was not, explain where you made your mistake.

Exercise 2:
```
32
0
```

Was your answer completely correct? If it was not, can you explain where you made your mistake?

Exercise 3:
```
0
-17
```

Was your answer completely correct? If it was not, can you explain where you made your mistake?

Exercise 4 :   The answers are T, T, and T.

Exercise 5: The answers are T, T, F, F, and F.

SELF CHECK #2

Exercise 1: Sum is 44

Were they correct? If not, do you know why not?

Exercise 2: The loop in program `Count` is a count-controlled loop because the loop body is executed a specified number of times.

Exercise 3: Sum is 16

Was your answer correct? If not, do you know why not?

Exercise 4: The loop in program `Count2` is an event-controlled loop because input of a negative data value (the event) stops it.

SELF CHECK #3

Exercise 1:
```
100
100
100
```

Were your answers correct? If not, do you understand your mistakes?

Exercise 2: While loops and For loops are pretest loops; the loop body is not executed if the ending condition is true initially.   Do-While loops are posttest loops; their bodies are always executed at least once.

Exercise 3:
```
5 + -7 is -2
-5 + -8 is -13
7 - 7 is 0
8 -  -8 is 16
```

Were your answers correct? If not, do you understand your mistakes?

Exercise 4: If a lowercase *Q* is entered, the body of the While statement is executed again. The screen freezes waiting for you to enter more values.

Chapter 3

SELF CHECK #1

Exercise 1:
```
The next line contains 10 stars.
**********
**********
```

Were you correct? If not, explain your error. (Did the output statement mislead you? What should the output statement say?)

Exercise 2:
```
The area of the 10 by 23 rectangle is 230
```

Exercise 3:
```
The area of the 23 by 10 rectange is 230.
```

SELF CHECK #2

Exercise 1:
```
Output from first call to SumNumbers
Sum is 100
Output from second call to SumNumbers
Sum is 0
```

Were your answers correct? If not, can you explain what you did wrong?

Exercise 2: `counter`, `sum`, `number`, `inNums`, and `SumNumbers`.

Exercise 3:

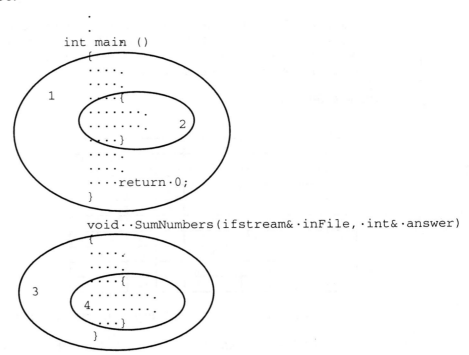

Exercise 4: Block 1 has no local identifiers.   Block 2 has local identifier **sum**, which hides global identifier **sum**. Block 3 has three local identifiers: **inFile, answer**, and **counter**.

Exercise 5: automatic local variable: **sum** (local to 2). All parameters also are automatic variables.

Exercise 6: static local variable: **counter** (local to 3). All global variables also are static.

Chapter 4

SELF CHECK #1

Exercise 1:
```
Pressure in normal range.
Pressure in normal range.
Pressure in normal range.
Pressure on the high side.
Pressure on the high side.
Error in input.
Evacuate plant!!!!
```

Was your answer correct? If not, so you know what calculated incorrectly?

SELF CHECK #2

Exercise 1: Sum is 30

Was your answer correct? If not, do you understand what you did wrong?

Exercise 2: C++ doesn't define what happens if you store more values than there are places in the array. Each system handles this differently. For example, on one system, the program may work correctly while on another system the program may crash. The moral is: don't do it.

SELF CHECK #3

Exercise 1:

–	–	–	–	–	*	*	*	*	*
–	–	–	–	–	*	*	*	*	*
–	–	–	–	–	*	*	*	*	*
–	–	–	–	–	*	*	*	*	*
–	–	–	–	–	*	*	*	*	*
*	*	*	*	*	+	+	+	+	+
*	*	*	*	*	+	+	+	+	+
*	*	*	*	*	+	+	+	+	+
*	*	*	*	*	+	+	+	+	+
*	*	*	*	*	+	+	+	+	+

Was your diagram correct? If not, do you understand what you did wrong?

Exercise 2: The first loop is processing by column; the second by row; the third by column.

Appendixes

Appendix A   Reserved Words

The following identifiers are *reserved words*—identifiers with predefined meanings in the C++ language. The programmer cannot declare them for other uses in a C++ program.

asm	double	new	switch
auto	else	operator	template
break	enum	private	this
case	extern	protected	throw
catch	float	public	try
char	for	register	typedef
class	friend	return	union
const	goto	short	unsigned
continue	if	signed	virtual
default	inline	sizeof	void
delete	int	static	volatile
do	long	struct	while

Appendix B   Operator Precedence

The following is a complete list of the C++ operators, some of which are not covered in the manual. Operators are binary unless marked unary.

Operators	Associativity
: :	Left to right
( ) [ ] -> .	Left to right
++ -- ~ ! + - & * **new** (unary)	Right to left
delete (cast) **sizeof** (unary)	Right to left
->* .*	Left to right
* / %	Left to right
+ -	Left to right
<< >>	Left to right
< <= > >=	Left to right
== !=	Left to right
&	Left to right
^	Left to right
|	Left to right
& &	Left to right
| |	Left to right
? :	Right to left

```
=  +=  -+  etc.                                  Right to left
,  (the operator, not the separator)             Left to right
```

Appendix C   Description of Selected Operators

Type of Operator	*Operator*	*Meaning*
arithmetic	*	Unary plus
	-	Unary minus
	+	Addition
	-	Subtraction
	*	Multiplication
	/	Floating point operands: floating point result Integer operands: quotient Mixed operands: floating point result
	%	Modulus (remainder from integer division, operands must be integral)
	++	Increment by one; can be prefix or postfix
	--	Decrement by one; can be prefix or postfix
	sizeof	returns the size in bytes of its operand
assignment	=	Assignment; evaluate expression on the right and store in variable named on the left
I/O	<<	Insertion; insert the characters (if a string) or the value (if a variable or constant) in the output stream named on the left of the first insertion operator
	>>	Extraction; extract the value from the input stream named on the left of the first extraction operator and store in the place named on the right
relational	==	Equal to
	!=	Not equal to
	>	Greater than
	<	Less than
	>=	Greater than or equal to
	<=	Less than or equal to
logical	&&	AND is a binary Boolean operator. If both operands are true, the result is true. Otherwise, the result is false.

logical (cont.)	||	OR is a binary Boolean operator. If at least one of the operands is true, the result is true. Otherwise, the result is false.
	!	NOT is a unary Boolean operator. NOT changes the value of its operand: if the operand is true, the result is false; if the operand is false, the result it true.
pointer related	*	(postfix on a type or prefix on a variable in a pointer variable declaration) Declare a variable that is a *pointer to* a place that can contain a variable of the type; must be dereferenced to access the place pointed to
	*	(prefix on a pointer variable in an expression) Dereferencing operator; accesses *place pointed to*
	&	(postfix on a type or prefix on a variable in a reference variable declaration) Declare a variable that is a *pointer to* a place that can contain a variable of the type; dereferenced automatically by the compiler
	&	(prefix on a variable) *Address of* a variable
	->	(infix between a pointer variable to **struct** or **class** and member name) Dereferences a pointer variable and accesses a member
	new	Returns the address of new space allocated for a dynamic variable of the type named on the right
	delete	Returns the space allocated for the dynamic variable on the right to the heap to be allocated again
selection	.	(infix: **struct** variable.member) Accesses the member field of the **struct** variable
	.	(infix: **class** variable.member) Accesses the member data or function of the **class** variable
	[ ]	(postfix: encloses an integral expression) Accesses a position within the array variable named on the left
scope resolution	::	(infix: **class** type::method) Associates a method with the **class** in which it is declared

Appendix D C++ Library Routines and Constants

Header File **ctype.h**

isalnum(ch)	Returns true if **ch** is a letter or a digit; false otherwise.
isalpha(ch)	Returns true if **ch** is a letter; false otherwise.
iscntrl(ch)	Returns true if **ch** is a control character; false, otherwise.
isdigit(ch)	Returns true if **ch** is a digit; false otherwise.
isgraph(ch)	Returns true if **ch** is a nonblank printable character; false otherwise.
islower(ch)	Returns true if **ch** is lowercase; false otherwise.
isprint(ch)	Returns true if **ch** is a printable character; false otherwise.
ispunct(ch)	Returns true if **ch** is a nonblank printable character (i.e., not a letter or a digit); false otherwise.
isspace(ch)	Returns true if **ch** is a whitespace character; false otherwise.
isupper(ch)	Returns true if **ch** is an uppercase letter; false otherwise.
toupper(ch)	Returns **ch** in uppercase regardless of original case.
tolower(ch)	Returns **ch** in lowercase regardless of original case.

Header File **string.h**

strcat(s1, s2)	Returns the base address of **s1** with **s2** concatenated on the end.
strcmp(s1, s2)	Returns a negative integer if **s1** comes before **s2**; returns zero if **s1** is equal to **s2**; and returns a positive integer if **s2** comes before **s1**.
strcpy(s1, s2)	returns the base address of **s1** with **s2** copied in it.
strlen(s)	Returns the number of characters in **s**.

Header File **stddef.h**

NULL	The system-dependent null pointer constant (usually 0).

Header File **float.h**

FLT_DIG	Approximate number of significant digits in a **float** value on your machine.
FLT_MAX	Maximum positive **float** value on your machine.
FLT_MIN	Minimum positive **float** value on your machine.
DBL_DIG	Approximate number of significant digits in a **double** value on your machine.
DBL_MAX	Maximum positive **double** value on your machine.
DBL_MIN	Minimum positive **double** value on your machine.
LDBL_DIG	Approximate number of significant digits in a **long double** value on your machine.
LDBL_MAX	Maximum positive **long double** value on your machine.
LDBL_MIN	Minimum positive **long double** value on your machine.

Header File `limits.h`

`CHAR_BITS`	Number of bits in a byte on your machine.
`CHAR_MAX`	Maximum **char** value on your machine.
`CHAR_MIN`	Minimum **char** value on your machine.
`SHRT_MAX`	Maximum **short** value on your machine.
`SHRT_MIN`	Minimum **short** value on your machine.
`INT_MAX`	Maximum **int** value on your machine.
`INT_MIN`	Minimum **int** value on your machine.
`LONG_MAX`	Maximum **long** value on your machine.
`LONG_MIN`	Minimum **long** value on your machine.
`UCHAR_MAX`	Maximum **unsigned char** value on your machine.
`USHRT_MAX`	Maximum **unsigned short** value on your machine.
`UINT_MAX`	Maximum **unsigned int** value on your machine.
`ULONG_MAX`	Maximum **unsigned long** value on your machine.

Appendix E   The Character Sets

The following charts show the ordering of the two most common character sets: ASCII (American Standard Code for Information Interchange) and EBCDIC (Extended Binary Coded Decimal Interchange Code). The internal representation for each character is shown in decimal. For example, the letter *A* is represented internally as the integer 65 in ASCII and as 193 in EBCDIC. The blank character is denoted by a "_".

ASCII

Left Digit(s)	*Right digit* 0	*1*	*2*	*3*	*4*	*5*	*6*	*7*	*8*	*9*
0	NUL	SOH	STX	ETX	EOT	ENQ	ACK	BEL	BS	HT
1	LF	VT	FF	CR	SO	SI	DLE	DC1	DC2	DC3
2	DC4	NAK	SYN	ETB	CAN	EM	SUB	ESC	FS	GS
3	RS	US	_	!	"	#	$	%	&	´
4	(	)	*	+	,	−	.	/	0	1
5	2	3	4	5	6	7	8	9	:	;
6	<	=	>	?	@	A	B	C	D	E
7	F	G	H	I	J	K	L	M	N	O
8	P	Q	R	S	T	U	V	W	X	Y
9	Z	[	\	]	^	_	_	a	b	c
10	d	e	f	g	h	i	j	k	l	m
11	n	o	p	q	r	s	t	u	v	w
12	x	y	z	{			}	~	DEL		

Codes 00-31 and 127 are the following nonprintable control characters:

NUL	Null character		LF	Line feed
SOH	Start of header		VT	Vertical tab
STX	Start of text		FF	Form feed
ETX	End of text		CR	Carriage return
EOT	End of transmission		SI	Shift in
ENQ	Enquiry		DLE	Data link escape
ACK	Acknowledge		DC1	Device control one
BEL	Bell character (beep)		DC2	Device control two
BS	Back space		DC3	Device control three
HT	Horizontal tab		DC4	Device control four

NAK Negative acknowledge
(ASCII control characters cont.)
SYN Synchronous idle
ETB End of transmitted block
CAN Cancel
EM   End of medium
SUB Substitute

ESC Escape
FS   File separator
GS   Group separator
RS   Record separator
US   Unit separator
DEL Delete

EBCDIC

Left Digit(s)	Right Digit 0	1	2	3	4	5	6	7	8	9
6					–					
7					¢	.	<	(	+	|
8	&									
9	!	$	*	)	;	¬	–	/		
10							^	,	%	_
11	>	?								
12		`	:	#	@	´	=	"		a
13	b	c	d	e	f	g	h	i		
14						j	k	l	m	n
15	o	p	q	r						
16		~	s	t	u	v	w	x	y	z
17								\	{	}
18	[	]								
19				A	B	C	D	E	F	G
20	H	I								J
21	K	L	M	N	O	P	Q	R		
22							S	T	U	V
23	W	X	Y	Z						
24	0	1	2	3	4	5	6	7	8	9

Nonprintable control characters—codes 00–63, 250–255, and those for which empty spaces appear in the chart—are not shown.

Glossary

abstract data type   a class of data objects with a defined set of properties and a set of operations that process the data objects while maintaining the properties

abstract step   an algorithmic step for which some implementation details remain unspecified

abstraction   a model of a complex system that includes only the details essential to the perspective of the viewer of the system; the separation of the logical properties of data or actions from their implementation details

abstraction (in OOD)   the essential characteristics of an object from the viewpoint of the user

actual parameter   a variable, constant, or expression listed in the call to a function or procedure

aggregate operation   an operation on a data structure as a whole, as opposed to an operation on an individual component of the data structure

algorithm   a logical sequence of discrete steps that describes a complete solution to a given problem computable in a finite amount of time; a step-by-step procedure for solving a problem in a finite amount of time; a verbal or written description of a logical sequence of actions

ALU   see *arithmetic/logic unit*

anonymous type   a user-defined type that does not have an identifier (a name) associated with it

arithmetic/logic unit (ALU)   the component of the central processing unit that performs arithmetic and logical operations

array data type   a collection of components, all of the same type, ordered on N dimensions ($N >= 1$); each component is accessed by N indices, each of which represents the component's position within that dimension

assembler   a program that translates an assembly language program into machine code

assembly language   a low-level programming language in which a mnemonic represents each of the machine language instructions for a particular computer

assertion A logical proposition that is either true or false

assignment expression   a C++ expression with a value and the side effect of storing the expression value into a memory location

assignment statement   a statement that stores the value of an expression into a variable

atomic data type   a data type that allows only a single value to be associated with an identifier of that type

automatic variable   a variable for which memory is allocated and deallocated when control enters and exits the block in which it is declared

auxiliary storage device   a device that stores data in encoded form outside the computer's memory

base case   the case for which the solution can be stated nonrecursively

base class   the class being inherited from

big-O notation   a notation that expresses computing time (complexity) as the term in a function that increases most rapidly relative to the size of a problem

binary   expressed in terms of combinations of the numbers 1 and 0 only

binary search   a search algorithm for sorted lists that involves dividing the list in half and determining, by value comparison, whether the item would be in the upper or lower half; the process is performed repeatedly until either the item is found or it is determined that the item is not on the list

bit   short for binary digit; a single 1 or 0

block   in C++, a group of zero or more statements enclosed in braces

body   the statement(s) to be repeated within the loop; the executable statement(s) within a function

Boolean   a data type consisting of only two values: true and false

Boolean expression   an assertion that is evaluated as either true or false, the only values of the Boolean data type

Boolean operators   operators applied to values of the type Boolean; in C++ these are the special symbols &&, | |, and !

booting the system the process of starting up a computer by loading the operating system into its main memory

branch a code segment that is not always executed; for example, a Switch statement has as many branches as there are case labels

branching control structure see *selection control structure*

byte eight bits

call the point at which the computer begins following the instructions in a subprogram is referred to as the subprogram call

cancellation error a form of representational error that occurs when numbers of widely differing magnitudes are added or subtracted

central processing unit (CPU) the part of the computer that executes the instructions (program) stored in memory; consists of the arithmetic/logic unit and the control unit

char data type whose values consist of one alphanumeric character (letter, digit, or special symbol)

character set a standard set of alphanumeric characters with a given collating sequence and binary representation

class an unstructured type that encapsulates a fixed number of data components with the functions that manipulate them; the predefined operations on an instance of a class are whole assignment and component access

class constructor a special member function of a class that is implicitly invoked when a class object is defined

class destructor a special member function of a class that is implicitly invoked when a class object goes out of scope

class member a component of a class; class members may be either data or functions

class object (class instance) a variable of a class type

client software that declares and manipulates objects (instances) of a particular class

code walk-through a verification process for a program in which each statement is examined to check that it faithfully implements the corresponding algorithmic step, and that the preconditions and postconditions of each module are preserved

coding translating an algorithm into a programming language; the process of assigning bit patterns to pieces of information

collating sequence the ordering of the elements of a set or series, such as the characters (values) in a character set

compiler a program that translates a high-level language (such as C++, Pascal, or FORTRAN) into machine code

compiler listing a copy of a program into which have been inserted messages from the compiler (indicating errors in the program that prevent its translation into machine language if appropriate)

complexity a measure of the effort expended by the computer in performing a computation, relative to the size of the computation

composite type a data type that allows a collection of values to be associated with an object of that type

composition (containment) a mechanism by which an internal data member of one class is defined to be an object of another class type

computer a programmable device that can store, retrieve, and process data

computer program a list of instructions to be performed by a computer

computer programming the process of planning a sequence of steps for a computer to follow

concrete step a step for which the implementation details are fully specified

conditional test the point at which the Boolean expression is evaluated and the decision is made to either begin a new iteration or skip to the first statement following the loop

constant an item in a program whose value is fixed at compile time and cannot be changed during execution

constant time an algorithm whose Big-O work expression is a constant

control abstraction the separation of the logical properties of a control structure from its implementation

control structure a statement used to alter the normally sequential flow of control

control unit the component of the central processing unit that controls the action of other components so that instructions (the program) are executed in sequence

conversion function a function that converts a value of one type to another type so that it can be assigned to a variable of the second type; also called transfer function or type cast

copy-constructor a special member function of a class that is implicitly invoked when passing parameters by value, initializing a variable in a declaration, and returning an object as the value of a function

count-controlled loop a loop that executes a predetermined number of times

counter a variable whose value is incremented to keep track of the number of times a process or event occurs

CPU see *central processing unit*

crash the cessation of a computer's operations as a result of the failure of one of its components; cessation of program execution to an error due to an error

cursor control keys a special set of keys on a computer keyboard that allow the user to move the cursor up, down, right, and left to any point on the screen

data information that has been put into a form a computer can use

data abstraction the separation of a data type's logical properties from its implementation

data encapsulation the separation of the representation of data from the applications that use the data at a logical level; a programming language feature that enforces information hiding

data flow the flow of information from the calling code to a function and from the function back to the calling code

data representation the concrete form of data used to represent the abstract values of an abstract data type

data structure a collection of data elements whose organization is characterized by accessing operations that are used to store and retrieve the individual data elements; the implementation of the composite data members in an abstract data type

data type the general form of a class of data items; a formal description of the set of values (called the domain) and the basic set of operations that can be applied to it

data validation a test added to a program or a function that checks for errors in the data

debugging the process by which errors are removed from a program so that it does exactly what it is supposed to do

decision see *selection control structure*

declaration a statement that associates an identifier with a process or object so that the

user can refer to that process or object by name

deep copy an operation that not only copies one class object to another but also makes copies of any pointed-to data

delete a C++ operator that returns the space allocated for a dynamic variable back to the heap to be used again

demotion (narrowing) the conversion of a value from a "higher" type to a "lower" type according to a programming language's precedence of data types. Demotion may cause loss of information

dereference operator an operator that when applied to a pointer variable denotes the variable to which the pointer points

derived class   the class that inherits

deskchecking tracing an execution of a design or program on paper

development environment a single package containing all of the software required for developing a program

documentation the written text and comments that make a program easier for others to understand, use, and modify

down a descriptive term applied to a computer when it is not in a usable condition

driver a simple dummy main program that is used to call a function being tested; a main function in an object-oriented program

dynamic allocation allocation of memory space for a variable at run time (as opposed to static allocation at compile time)

dynamic binding the run-time determination of which implementation of an operation is appropriate

dynamic data structure a data structure that can expand and contract during program execution

dynamic variable a variable created during execution of a program by the new operator

echo printing printing the data values input to a program to verify that they are correct

editor an interactive program used to create and modify source programs or data

encapsulation (in OOD) the bundling of data and actions in such a way that the logical properties of the data and actions are separated from the implementation details; the practice of hiding a module implementation in a separate block with a formally specified interface

enumeration data type a data type in which the formal description of the set of values is an ordered list of literal values

enumerator one of the values in the domain of an enumeration type

event counter a variable that is incremented each time a particular event occurs

event-controlled loop a loop that terminates when something happens inside the loop body to signal that the loop should be exited

executing the action of a computer performing as instructed by a given program

execution trace a testing procedure that involves simulating by hand the computer executing a program

expression an arrangement of identifiers, literals, and operators that can be evaluated to compute a value of a given type

expression statement a statement formed by appending a semicolon to an expression

external file a file that is used to communicate with people or programs and is stored externally to the program

external pointer a named pointer variable that references the first node in a linked list

external representation the printable (character) form of a data value

fetch-execute cycle the sequence of steps performed by the central processing unit for each machine language instruction

field a group of character positions in a line of output

field identifier (member identifier in C++) the name of a component in a record (struct)

field of a record a component of a record data type

field member selector the expression used to access components of a record variable; formed by using the record variable name and the field identifier, separated by a period

file a named area in secondary storage that is used to hold a collection of data; the collection of data itself

finite state machine an idealized model of a simple computer consisting of a set of states, the rules that specify when states are changed, and a set of actions that are performed when changing states

flag a Boolean variable that is set in one part of the program and tested in another to control the logical flow of a program

flat implementation the hierarchical structure of a solution written as one long sequence of steps; also called inline implementation

floating point number the value stored in a type `float` variable, so called because part of the memory location holds the exponent and the balance of the location the mantissa, with the decimal point floating as necessary among the significant digits

flow of control the order of execution of the statements in a program

formal parameter a variable declared in a function heading

formal parameter declaration the code that associates a formal parameter identifier with a data type and a passing mechanism

formatting the planned positioning of statements or declarations and blanks on a line of a program; the arranging of program output so that it is neatly spaced and aligned

free store (heap) A pool of memory locations reserved for dynamic allocation of data

function a subprogram in C++

function call an expression or statement in the main program requiring the computer to execute a function subprogram

function definition ta function declaration that includes the body of the function

function prototype a function declaration without the body of the function

function result the value computed by the function and then returned to the main program; often just called the result

function result type the data type of the result value returned by a function; often referred to simply as function type

function type see *function result type*

functional cohesion a property of a module in which all concrete steps are directed toward solving just one problem, and any significant subproblems are written as abstract steps

functional equivalence a property of a module that performs exactly the same operation as the abstract step it defines, or when one module performs exactly the same operation as another module

functional modules in top-down design, the structured tasks and subtasks that are solved individually to create an effective program

functional problem description a description that clearly states what a program is to do

general (recursive) case the case for which the solution is expressed in terms of a smaller version of itself

global a descriptive term applied to an identifier declared outside any function, so-called because it is accessible to everything that follows it

hardware the physical components of a computer

heuristics assorted problem-solving strategies

hierarchical implementation a process in which a modular solution is implemented by subprograms that duplicate the hierarchical structure of the solution

hierarchical records records in which at least one of the fields is itself a record

hierarchy (in OOD) structuring of abstractions in which a descendant object inherits the characteristics of its ancestors

high-level programming language any programming language in which a single statement translates into one or more machine language instructions

homogeneous a descriptive term applied to structures in which all components are of the same data type (such as an array)

identifier a name associated with a process or object and used to refer to that process or object

implementation phase the second set of steps in programming a computer: translating (coding) the algorithm into a programming language; testing the resulting program by running it on a computer, checking for accuracy, and making any necessary corrections; using the program

implementing coding and testing an algorithm

implementing a test plan running the program with the test cases listed in the test plan

implicit matching see *positional matching*

in place describes a kind of sorting algorithm in which the components in an array are sorted without the use of a second array

index a value that selects a component of an array

infinite loop a loop whose termination condition is never reached and which therefore is never exited without intervention from outside of the program

infinite recursion the situation in which a subprogram calls itself over and over continuously

information any knowledge that can be communicated

information hiding The practice of hiding the details of a function or data structure with the goal of controlling access to the details

of a module or structure; the programming technique of hiding the details of data or actions from other parts of the program

inheritance A design technique used with a hierarchy of classes by which each descendant class inherits the properties (data and operations) of its ancestor class; the language mechanism by which one class acquires the properties—data and operations—of another class; a mechanism for automatically sharing data and methods among members of a class and its subclasses

inline implementation see *flat implementation*

input the process of placing values from an outside data set into variables in a program; the data may come from either an input device (keyboard) or an auxiliary storage device (disk or tape)

input prompts messages printed by an interactive program, explaining what data is to be entered

input transformation an operation that takes input values and converts them to the abstract data type representation

input/output (I/O) devices the parts of a computer that accept data to be processed (input) and present the results of that processing (output)

integer number a positive or negative whole number made up of a sign and digits (when the sign is omitted, a positive sign is assumed)

interactive system a system that allows direct communication between the user and the computer

interface a connecting link (such as a computer terminal) at a shared boundary that allows independent systems (such as the user and the computer) to meet and act on or communicate with each other; the formal definition of the behavior of a subprogram and the mechanism for communicating with it

internal file a file that is created but not save; also called a scratch file

interpreter a program that inputs a program in a high-level language and directs the computer to perform the actions specified in each statement; unlike a compiler, and interpreter does not produce a machine language version of the entire program

invoke to call on a subprogram, causing the subprogram to execute before control is returned to the statement following the call

iteration an individual pass through, or repetition of, the body of a loop

iteration counter a counter variable that is incremented with each iteration of a loop

iterator an operation that allows us to process all the components in an abstract data type sequentially

length the actual number of values stored in a list or string

lifetime the period of time during program execution when an identifier has memory allocated to it

linear time for an algorithm, when the Big-O work expression can be expressed in terms of a constant times N, where N is the number of values in a data set

linked list a list in which the order of the components is determined by an explicit link field in each node, rather than by the sequential order of the components in memory

listing a copy of a source program, output by a compiler, containing messages to the programmer

literal value any constant value written in a program

local variable a variable declared within a block; it is not accessible outside of that block

logarithmic order for an algorithm, when the Big-O work expression can be expressed in terms of the logarithm of N, where N is the number of values in a data set

logging off informing a computer—usually through a simple command—that no further commands follow

logging on taking the preliminary steps necessary to identify yourself to a computer so that it accept your commands

logical order the order in which the programmer wants the statements in the program to be executed, which may differ from the physical order in which they appear

loop a method of structuring statements so that they are repeated while certain conditions are met

loop control variable (LCV) a variable whose value is used to determine whether the loop executes another iteration or exits

loop entry the point at which the flow of control first passes to a statement inside a loop

loop exit that point when the repetition of the loop body ends and control passes to the first statement following the loop

loop invariant assertions about the characteristics of a loop that must always be true for a loop to execute properly; the assertions are true on loop entry, at the start of each loop iteration, and on exit from the loop, but are not necessarily true at each point in the body of the loop

loop test the point at which the loop expression is evaluated and the decision is made either to begin a new iteration or skip to the statement immediately following the loop

machine language the language, made up of binary-coded instructions, that is used directly by the computer

mainframe a large computing system designed for high-volume processing or for use by many people at once

maintenance the modification of a program, after it has been completed, in order to meet changing requirements or to take care of any errors that show up

maintenance phase period during which maintenance occurs

mantissa with respect to floating point representation of real numbers, the digits representing a number itself and not its exponent

member selector the expression used to access components of a `struct` or `class` variable. It is formed by using the variable name and the member name, separated by a dot (period)

memory leak the loss of available memory space that occurs when memory are allocated dynamically but never deallocated

memory unit internal data storage in a computer

metalanguage a language that is used to write the syntax rules for another language

method a function declared as a member of a class object

microcomputer see *personal computer*

minicomputer a computer system larger than a personal computer but smaller than a mainframe; sometimes called an entry-level mainframe

mixed mode expression an expression that contains operands of different data types

modular programming see *top-down design*

modularity (in OOD) meaningful packaging of objects

module a self-contained collection of steps that solves a problem or subproblem; can contain both concrete and abstract steps

module nesting chart a chart that depicts the nesting structure of modules and shows calls among them

name precedence the priority treatment accorded a local identifier in a block over a global identifier with the same spelling in any references that the block makes to that identifier

named constant a location in memory, referenced by an identifier, where a data value that cannot be changed is stored

named type a type that has an identifier (a name) associated with it

nested control structure a program structure consisting of one control statement (selection, iteration, or subprogram) embedded within another control statement

nested If an If statement that is nested within another If statement

nested loop a loop that is within another loop

new a C++ operator that returns the address of new space allocated for a dynamic variable

nodes the building blocks of dynamic structures, each made up of a component (the data) and a pointer (the link) to the next node

nonlocal a descriptive term applied to any identifier declared outside of a given block

nonlocal access access to any identifier declared outside of its own block

null statement an empty statement

nybble four bits; half of a byte

object class (class) the description of a group of objects with similar properties and behaviors; a pattern for creating individual objects

object program the machine-language version of a source program

object-based programming language a programming language that supports abstraction and encapsulation, but not inheritance

object-oriented design a building-block design technique that incorporates abstraction, encapsulation, modularity, and hierarchy

object-oriented programming a method of implementation in which programs are organized as cooperative collections of objects, each of which represents an instance of some class, and whose classes are all members of a hierarchy of classes united via inheritance relationships

observer an operation that allows us to observe the state of an instance of an abstract data type without changing it

one-dimensional array a structured collection of components of the same type given a single name; each component is accessed by an index that indicates its position within the collection

operating system a set of programs that manages all of the computer's resources

out-of-bounds array index an index value that, in C++, is either less than zero or greater than the array size minus one

output transformation an operation that takes an instance of an abstract data type and converts it to a representation that can be output

overflow the condition that arises when the value of a calculation is too large to be represented

overloading giving the same name to more than one function or using the same operator symbol for more than one operation; usually associated with static binding

overriding reimplementing a member function inherited from a parent class

parameter a literal, constant, variable, or expression used for communicating values to or from a subprogram

parameter list a mechanism by which functions communicate with each other

pass by address a parameter-passing mechanism in which the memory address of the actual parameter is passed to the formal parameter; also called pass by reference

pass by name a parameter-passing mechanism in which the actual parameter is passed to a function as a literal character string and interpreted by a thunk

pass by reference see *pass by address*

pass by value a parameter-passing mechanism in which a copy of an actual parameter's value is passed to the formal parameter

password a unique series of letters assigned to a user (and known only by that user) by which that user identifies himself or herself to a computer during the logging-on procedure; a password system protects information stored in a computer from being tampered with or destroyed

path a combination of branches that might be traversed when a program or function is executed

path testing a testing technique whereby the tester tries to execute all possible paths in a program or function

PC see *personal computer*

peripheral device an input, output, or auxiliary storage device attached to a computer

personal computer (PC) a small computer system (usually intended to fit on a desktop) that is designed to be used primarily by a single person

pointer a simple data type consisting of an unbounded set of values, each of which addresses or otherwise indicates the location of a variable of a given type; operations defined on pointer variables are assignment and test for equality

polymorphic operation an operation that has multiple meanings depending on the type of the object to which it is bound at run time

polymorphism The ability to determine which of several operations with the same name is appropriate; a combination of static and dynamic binding

positional matching a method of matching actual and formal parameters by their relative positions in the two parameter lists; also called *relative* or *implicit* matching

postconditions assertions that must be true after a module is executed

postfix operator an operator that follows its operand(s)

precision a maximum number of significant digits

preconditions assertions that must be true before a module begins execution

prefix operator an operator that precedes its operand(s)

priming read an initial reading of a set of data values before entry into an event-controlled loop in order to establish values for the variables

problem-solving phase the first set of steps in programming a computer: analyzing the problem; developing an algorithm; testing the algorithm for accuracy

procedural abstraction the separation of the logical properties of an action from its implementation

programming planning, scheduling, or performing a task or an event; see also *computer programming*

programming language a set of rules, symbols, and special words used to construct a program

pseudocode a mixture of English statements and C++-like control structures that can easily by translated into a programming language

range of values the interval within which values must fall, specified in terms of the largest and smallest allowable values

real number a number that has a whole and a fractional part and no imaginary part

record (struct) data type a composite data type with a fixed number of components called fields (members); the operations are whole record assignment and selection of individual fields by name

recursion the situation in which a subprogram calls itself

recursive call a subprogram call in which the subprogram being called is the same as the one making the call

recursive case see *general case*

recursive definition a definition in which something is defined in terms of a smaller version of itself

reference parameter a formal parameter that receives the location (memory address) of the caller's actual parameter

reference type a simple data type consisting of an unbounded set of values, each of which is the address of a variable of a given type. The only operation defined on a reference variable is initialization, after which every appearance of the variable is implicitly dereferenced

refinement in top-down design, the expansion of a module specification to form a new module that solves a major step in the computer solution of a problem

relational operators operators that state that a relationship exists between two values; in C++, symbols that cause the computer to perform operations to verify whether or not the indicated relationship exists

representational error arithmetic error caused when the precision of the true result of arithmetic operations is greater than the precision of the machine

reserved word a word that has special meaning in a programming language; it cannot be used as an identifier

result see *function result*

return the point at which the computer comes back from executing a function

right-justified placed as far to the right as possible within a fixed number of character positions

robust a descriptive term for a program that can recover from erroneous inputs and keep running

run-time stack a data structure that keeps track of activation records during the execution of a program

scope the region of program code where it is legal to reference (use) an identifier

scope rules the rules that determine where in a program a given identifier may be accessed, given the point at which the identifier is declared

scratch file see *internal file*

secondary storage device see *auxiliary storage device*

selection control structure a form of program structure allowing the computer to select one among possible actions to perform based on given circumstances; also called a *branching control structure*

self the instance object (class) used in the invocation of a method

self-documenting code a program containing meaningful identifiers as well as judiciously used clarifying comments

semantics the set of rules that gives the meaning of instruction written in a programming language

semihierarchical implementation a modular solution implemented by functions in a manner that preserves the hierarchical design, except that a function used by multiple modules is im-plemented once, outside of the hierarchy, and called in each place it is needed

sentinel a special data value used in certain event-controlled loops as a signal that the loop should be exited

sequence a structure in which statements are executed one after another

shallow copy an operation that copies one class object to another without copying any pointed-to data

side effect any effect of one function on another that is not part of the explicitly defined interface between them

significant digits those digits from the first nonzero digit on the left to the last nonzero digit on the right (plus any zero digits that are exact)

simulation a problem solution that has been arrived at through the application of an algorithm designed to model the behavior of physical systems, materials, or processes

size (of an array) the physical space reserved for an array

software computer programs; the set of all programs available on a computer

software engineering the application of traditional engineering methodologies and techniques to the development of software

software life cycle the phases in the life of a large software project including requirements analysis, specification, design, implementation, testing, and maintenance

software piracy the unauthorized copying of software for either personal use or use by others

sorting arranging the components of a list in order (for instance, words in alphabetical order, numbers in ascending or descending order)

source program a program written in a high-level programming language

stable sort a sorting algorithm that preserves the order of duplicates

stack frame see *activation record*

standardized made uniform; most high-level languages are standardized, as official descriptions of them exist

static binding the compile-time determination of which function to call for a particular object

static variable a variable for which memory remains allocated throughout the execution of the entire program

stepwise design see *top-down design*

stepwise refinement see *top-down design*

string a collection of characters that is interpreted as a single data item; in C++, a null-terminated sequence of characters stored in a `char` array

stub a dummy function that assists in testing part of a program; it has the same function that would actually be called by the part of the program being tested, but is usually much simpler

style the individual manner in which computer programmers translate algorithms into a programming language

subprogram see *function*

supercomputer the most powerful class of computers

switch expression the expression in a Switch statement whose value determines which case label is selected. It cannot be a floating point expression

syntax the formal rules governing how valid instructions (constructs) are written in a programming language

system software a set of programs—including the compiler, the operating system, and the editor—that improves the efficiency and convenience of the computer's processing

tail recursion a recursive algorithm in which no statements are executed after the return from the recursive call

team programming the use of two or more programmers to design a program that would take one programmer too long to complete

temporary file a file that exists only during the execution of a program

termination condition the condition that causes a loop to be exited

test driver see *driver*

test plan a document that specifies how a program is to be tested

test plan implementation using the test cases specified in a test plan to verify that a program outputs the predicted results

testing checking a program's output by comparing it to hand-calculated results; running a program with data sets designed to discover any errors

text file a file in which each component is a character; each numeric digit is represented by its code in the collating sequence

top-down design a technique for developing a program in which the problem is divided into more easily handled subproblems, the solutions of which create a solution to the overall problem; also called stepwise refinement and modular programming

transfer function see *conversion function*

transformer an operation that builds a new value of an ADT, given one or more previous values of the type

traverse a list to access the components of a list one at a time from the beginning of the list to the end

two-dimensional array a collection of components, all of the same type, structured in two dimensions; each component is accessed by a pair of indices that represent the component's position within each dimension

type cast see *conversion function*

type coercion an automatic conversion of a value of one type to a value of another type

type definition the association of a type identifier with the definition of a new data type

unary operator an operator that has just one operand

underflow the condition that arises when the value of a calculation is too small to be represented

unstructured data type a collection consisting of components that are not organized with respect to one another

user name the name by which a computer recognizes the user, and which must be entered to log on to a machine

value parameter a formal parameter that receives a copy of the contents of the corresponding actual parameter

value-returning function a function that returns a single value to its caller and is invoked from within an expression

variable a location in memory, referenced by an identifier, in which a data value that can be changed is stored

virtual function a function in which each invocation cannot be matched with the proper code until run time

virus a computer program that replicates itself, often with the goal of spreading to other computers without authorization, possibly with the intent of doing harm

visible accessible; a term used in describing a scope of access

void function (procedure) a function that does not return a function value to its caller and is invoked as a separate statement

word a group of 16, 32, or 64 bits; a group of bits processed by the arithmetic-logic unit in a single instruction

work a measure of the effort expended by the computer in performing a computation

workstation a minicomputer or powerful microcomputr designed to be used primarily by one person at a time